AIA Guide
to Downtown
St. Paul

Publication of the

AIA Guide to Downtown St. Paul

has been made possible

through generous gifts from

AIA Minnesota

A Society of The American Institute of Architects

John R. Camp

George A. MacPherson Fund

Elmer L. and Eleanor Andersen Fund

Bean Family Fund for Business History

North Star Fund of the Minnesota Historical Society

Larry Millett

AIA Guide to Downtown St. Paul

Minnesota Historical Society Press

www.mhspress.org

The Minnesota Historical Society Press is a member of the Association of American University Presses.

10 9 8 7 6 5 4 3 2 1

International Standard Book Number
ISBN-13: 978-0-87351-721-8 (paper)
ISBN-10: 0-87351-721-0 (paper)

Library of Congress Cataloging-in-Publication Data
Millett, Larry, 1947–
       AIA guide to downtown St. Paul / Larry Millett.
       p.   cm.
Includes bibliographical references and index.
       ISBN-13: 978-0-87351-721-8 (pbk.)
       ISBN-10: 0-87351-721-0 (pbk.)
   1. Architecture—Minnesota—St. Paul—Guidebooks.
   2. St. Paul (Minn.)—Buildings, structures, etc.—Guidebooks.
   3. St. Paul (Minn.)—Guidebooks.
   I. Title.   II. Title: American Institute of Architects guide to downtown St. Paul.   III. Title: AIA guide to downtown Saint Paul.

NA735.S24M54   2010
720.9776'581—dc22

                                                                2009011263

Front cover: Landmark Center detail, Brian M. Gardner; Minnesota History Center detail, MHS; Brooks Building detail, Brian M. Gardner; F. Scott Fitzgerald statue, Jamie Maldonado; Science Museum of Minnesota detail, Brian M. Gardner

Back cover: Minnesota State Capitol dome, MHS; Pioneer Building light court and Ordway Center for the Performing Arts detail, Brian M. Gardner

Contents

Symbols Used in this Guidebook

! A building or place of exceptional architectural and/or historical significance

N Individually listed on the National Register of Historic Places or included within a National Register Historic District

L Locally designated as a historic property or within a local historic district

Abbreviations Used for Select Architectural Firms

ESG Architects	Elness, Swenson Graham Architects
HGA	Hammel, Green and Abrahamson
KKE Architects	Korsunsky Krank Erickson Architects
MS&R Architects	Meyer, Scherer and Rockcastle Architects
SOM	Skidmore, Owings and Merrill
TKDA	Toltz, King, Duvall, Anderson and Associates

Author's Note: This book is a revised, updated, and slighly expanded version of the chapter devoted to downtown St. Paul in my *AIA Guide to the Twin Cities*, published in 2007. Some entries here appear exactly as they are in that book; others have been changed to reflect new information or to provide additional historic background. I have also added a number of entries for buildings that either were omitted from the *AIA Guide* because of space limitations or have been built since its publication.

St. Paul Downtown

Map Area Enlarged

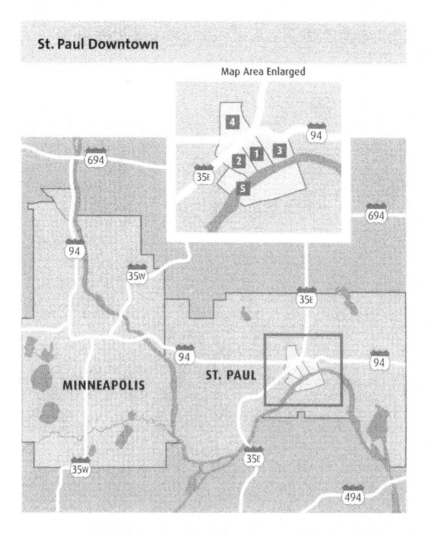

1 Central Core
2 Rice Park and Environs
3 Lowertown
4 State Capitol Area
5 The Near West Side, West Seventh Street,
  and Irvine Park

AIA Guide to Downtown St. Paul

Overview

Compared to its glitzy, skyscraper-laden competitor a few miles to the west, downtown St. Paul seems small and rather provincial. Its site, hemmed in by the Mississippi River and a ring of hills and steep bluffs, has always felt constricted, especially compared to the broad plain of downtown Minneapolis. Yet the site offered at least two key advantages for settlers who began drifting downriver from Fort Snelling in the 1830s. First, most of it was high enough above the river to be safe from flooding. Equally important, there were two steamboat landings (the so-called Lower Landing at the foot of Jackson Street and the Upper Landing at Chestnut Street) that could be reached with relative ease from the bluffs above. Geography in downtown St. Paul's case was indeed destiny, both for better and for worse.

Today, under even the most expansive definition of its boundaries, downtown St. Paul encompasses little more than a square mile, making it less than half the size of downtown Minneapolis. St. Paul's civic and business leaders recognized the problems posed by this compact site. Early in the twentieth century they went so far as to propose a plan for rerouting the Mississippi closer to the West Side bluffs, thereby creating more land for downtown growth. The plan never won federal approval.

For many years, downtown St. Paul also had a somewhat claustrophobic feel because of its narrow, crooked, and often confusing streets, which pioneer newspaper editor James Goodhue memorably described as the product of "a survey without measurement, a plan without method." The street system became especially bizarre near Seven Corners, where Sixth and Ninth originally followed a parallel course but were only a block apart. (If you're wondering what happened to Seventh and Eighth, well, it's a long story.) Over the years, streets have been widened, straightened, or even eliminated, and downtown St. Paul is now a model of clarity compared to what it once was. Even so, navigation can still prove perplexing to visitors from such exotic locales as Minneapolis.

Four distinct divisions characterize downtown St. Paul, which like Minneapolis features an extensive skyway system. In the center, naturally enough, is the commercial core, which extends back from the river bluffs between roughly St. Peter and Jackson streets. Office and government buildings dominate. To the west of St. Peter, where the downtown grid takes a sharp turn, is the Rice Park area, once more commonly known as Uppertown. Most of the city's cultural attractions, including the Ordway Center for the Performing Arts (1985) and the Science Museum of Minnesota (2000), are located here. East of Jackson Street is Lowertown, the city's historic warehouse district. As in Minneapolis, most of the old warehouses have been converted to apartments or offices. To the north, on a series of hills, is the State Capitol area, presided over by Cass Gilbert's magnificent white marble palace.

Although St. Paulites speak often and fondly of their city's devotion to historic preservation, this supposed trait is not overwhelmingly evident in the downtown core. Like Minneapolis and many other American cities, St. Paul embarked on an orgy of urban renewal in the 1960s, and over the following two decades much of downtown was utterly transformed. During the course of this upheaval, some of the city's most important nineteenth-century monuments were wantonly destroyed. Smaller Victorian-era commercial and institutional buildings also fell one by one, as did virtually all of downtown's remaining houses. With a few exceptions, the new buildings that rose from the ruins were mediocre at best and appallingly bad at worst.

Today, most of downtown St. Paul is a sleepy sort of place: only during the noon hour—when workers emerge from their cubicles and roam the skyways in search of food—does it have something like the pace and crackle of urban life. Part of the problem is that very little retail activity remains (only one department store, now owned by Macy's, lingers in the commercial district). Downtown's night life is also considerably less than scintillating, although the Seven Corners area does heat up on nights when the Minnesota Wild hockey team plays at the Xcel Energy Center (2000).

One positive trend has been the construction of a good deal of new and renovated housing, particularly in Lowertown. Downtown river-front development has also moved forward with such projects as the hugely popular—but architecturally uninspiring—Science Museum. The area around the historic Union Depot (1923) in Lowertown is also being championed as a future site for development along the river. However, St. Paul's peculiar geography—most of the downtown river-front is a narrow floodplain lodged beneath steep cliffs with railroad tracks and a highway running down the middle of it—will make development at water's edge very difficult.

Despite its dowdy image, downtown St. Paul offers much of archi-tectural interest, beginning with its extraordinary collection of major public buildings. Landmark Center (1892–1902), the Minnesota State Capitol (1905), the St. Paul Central Library and James J. Hill Reference Library (1917), and the St. Paul City Hall–Ramsey County Courthouse (1932) are nationally significant works of architecture, as is the immense St. Paul Cathedral (1915), which lords over all of downtown from the nearby heights of Summit Avenue.

Downtown St. Paul can also boast of two lovely little squares—Rice Park and Mears Park—as well as the Lowertown Historic District, home to over two dozen late nineteenth- and early twentieth-century brick warehouses, many of them of very high quality. Just to the west of Lowertown, along Robert Street, you'll find an outstanding group of late nineteenth-century office buildings, most notably the Pioneer Building (1889), which still has its original light court and open-cage elevators. Also of interest are such historic churches as Assumption Catholic (1874), First Baptist (1875), Central Presbyterian (1889), and St. Louis Catholic (1910). A pair of theaters—the Fitzgerald (1910) and the closed Orpheum (1916)—is all that remains of what was once a sizable entertainment district clustered around Seventh and Wabasha streets.

When it comes to modern architecture, downtown St. Paul is mostly meat and potatoes, although the quality of new buildings has improved since the drab days of the 1960s and 1970s. Still, you won't run across many examples of the sort of "starchitecture" that Minneapolis has long pursued. Two of downtown's finest modern buildings—Benjamin Thompson's visually pleasing but acoustically challenged Ordway Cen-ter and William Pedersen's headquarters building (1991) for Travelers Insurance Companies—are the work of native sons who went on to national prominence. But most of downtown's modern buildings, including the delightful Minnesota Children's Museum (1995) by Vincent James and Julie Snow, are the work of local architects.

1 The Central Core

The Central Core

Most of downtown's central core—an area bounded by the Mississippi River bluffs, Interstate 94, and St. Peter and Jackson streets—is part of the city's first plat, St. Paul Proper, surveyed in 1847 by brothers Ira and Benjamin Brunson. As plats go, there is nothing remarkable about it. The Brunsons laid out a standard gridiron, with numbered east-west streets running parallel to the river. The plat featured small blocks (about 300 feet square on average) and 60-foot-wide streets (tight by midwestern standards) and left no room for alleys, which would have been helpful. There was also no provision for parks, riverfront promenades, or other public amenities. It was, in short, a plat made mainly with the business of real estate speculation in mind.

As St. Paul began a period of spectacular growth in the 1880s, St. Paul Proper—originally the site of many small homes—quickly filled with commercial, retail, and industrial buildings. Among these were such prominent monuments as the Ryan Hotel (1885), the Globe Building (built in 1887 and designed by E. Townsend Mix, best known for his magnificent Metropolitan Building in Minneapolis), and the step-gabled New York Life Building (1889), one of the most distinctive skyscrapers of its era. Interspersed among these landmarks were scores of modest two- to six-story commercial buildings, usually clad in brick or stone and dating to 1900 or earlier.

Beginning in the late 1920s, the widening of Third Street to create Kellogg Boulevard removed many old buildings, but otherwise change came slowly to the central core through the first half of the twentieth century, largely because the city's stodgy growth rate did little to stimulate new development. As late as 1960, a visitor to this part of downtown would have found a virtual museum of nineteenth- and early twentieth-century commercial architecture. To be sure, it wasn't particularly pretty or quaint (many of the old buildings had been remodeled from the 1930s onward), and some blocks were downright shabby. Still, the downtown core in those days remained an undeniably *interesting* place, with the comfortably lived-in feel of a favorite old couch. It also functioned as a kind of anti-Minneapolis: a slow-paced, history-rich alternative to the Mill City's bustle and hustle.

Like almost all other American cities, however, St. Paul couldn't resist the urge to modernize, and by the early 1960s a great transformation of the central core began. An ambitious plan known as the Capital Centre project, backed by city government and the business community, served as the blueprint for redevelopment. The plan called for an array of new office towers and plazas, mostly along Fifth and Sixth streets, and it also introduced the mixed blessing of skyways to the downtown scene.

Over the next 20 years, the plan was carried out with ruthless enthusiasm. Numerous old buildings—among them some of the city's very best—came down, and new structures rose in their place, sometimes after a delay of many years. It all might have been worthwhile had the new work been of high quality, but that was seldom the case. The upheaval also had a devastating effect on the downtown retail trade. More than 200 stores left, and efforts to rebuild this lost retail base have proved futile.

Despite the damage done by years of urban renewal, this part of downtown has retained a number of important historic buildings, most notably the Pioneer-Endicott complex (1889–91) at Fourth and Robert streets. There are also some excellent modern buildings such as the Minnesota Children's Museum (1995). Overall, however, a walk through the central core provides a discouraging object lesson in how *not* to remake a city, best of intentions or no.

Kellogg Mall Park

POI A Kellogg Mall Park

South side of Kellogg Blvd. between Wabasha and Robert Sts.

1932 / rebuilt, St. Paul Parks Department (Tim Agness and Jody Martinez), 1991 / Art: fountains, sculptures, terra-cotta plaques, Cliff Garten, 1991

This park atop the downtown river bluffs was created as part of St. Paul's first big urban renewal project. Between 1929 and 1936, the city widened old Third St. and renamed it in honor of Frank B. Kellogg, a St. Paul lawyer who served as U.S. secretary of state in the 1920s and later won a Nobel Peace Prize. The mall, the project's centerpiece, was built to open up river views long blocked by buildings along Third. Forty-three buildings, some dating to the 1860s, were demolished to make way for the new boulevard and mall, obliterating what might be thought of as St. Paul's original "old town," comparable in some ways to Minneapolis's Gateway District. The park in its current guise dates to 1991, when it was completely redesigned. It's an inviting place, adorned with two fountains, sculptures executed at an odd tinker-toy scale, a pergola, and terra-cotta plaques, several depicting the inelegant puss of Pig's Eye Parrant, the whiskey-dealing reprobate who was among the city's founders. Below the mall, incidentally, is Second St. (originally Bench), which in earlier days provided a way up the bluff from the Lower Landing at the foot of Jackson St.

*LOST 1 Near the Robert St. end of the park a plaque marks the approximate site of the first **Chapel of St. Paul,** a log church built by Father Lucien Galtier in 1841. The city later took its name from this small structure.*

Wabasha Street Bridge

1 Wabasha Street Bridge

Across Mississippi River between downtown and the West Side

TKDA, James Carpenter and Associates (New York), and others, 1998 (opened)–2001 (overlooks completed)

The first bridge here was a wooden-truss structure that opened in 1859; at that time, only two other bridges—the Hennepin Avenue Suspension Bridge (1855) in Minneapolis and a railroad bridge (1856) at Rock Island, IL—spanned the Mississippi. The original bridge was replaced between 1889 and 1900 by a steel-truss span that stood until 1995, when it was knocked down to make way for a modern replacement.

New York artist James Carpenter, known for his sleek work in glass and metal, was selected to design the new bridge. Working with engineers, Carpenter in 1993 produced a spectacular proposal for a cable-stay structure

The Central Core

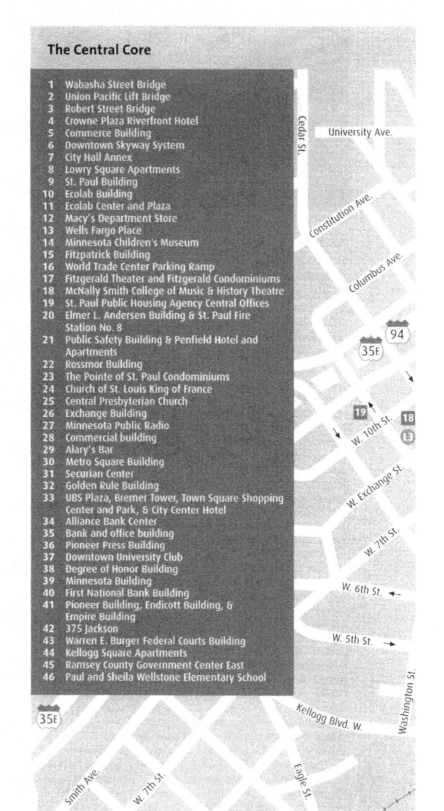

1   Wabasha Street Bridge
2   Union Pacific Lift Bridge
3   Robert Street Bridge
4   Crowne Plaza Riverfront Hotel
5   Commerce Building
6   Downtown Skyway System
7   City Hall Annex
8   Lowry Square Apartments
9   St. Paul Building
10 Ecolab Building
11 Ecolab Center and Plaza
12 Macy's Department Store
13 Wells Fargo Place
14 Minnesota Children's Museum
15 Fitzpatrick Building
16 World Trade Center Parking Ramp
17 Fitzgerald Theater and Fitzgerald Condominiums
18 McNally Smith College of Music & History Theatre
19 St. Paul Public Housing Agency Central Offices
20 Elmer L. Andersen Building & St. Paul Fire
    Station No. 8
21 Public Safety Building & Penfield Hotel and
    Apartments
22 Rossmor Building
23 The Pointe of St. Paul Condominiums
24 Church of St. Louis King of France
25 Central Presbyterian Church
26 Exchange Building
27 Minnesota Public Radio
28 Commercial building
29 Alary's Bar
30 Metro Square Building
31 Securian Center
32 Golden Rule Building
33 UBS Plaza, Bremer Tower, Town Square Shopping
    Center and Park, & City Center Hotel
34 Alliance Bank Center
35 Bank and office building
36 Pioneer Press Building
37 Downtown University Club
38 Degree of Honor Building
39 Minnesota Building
40 First National Bank Building
41 Pioneer Building, Endicott Building, &
    Empire Building
42 375 Jackson
43 Warren E. Burger Federal Courts Building
44 Kellogg Square Apartments
45 Ramsey County Government Center East
46 Paul and Sheila Wellstone Elementary School

A   Kellogg Mall Park
B   Remains of U.S. Quartermaster's
    Department Building
C   St. Paul Cultural Garden
D   Plaque: first Ramsey County
    Courthouse
E   Remnants of Hotel Spalding
F   Seventh Place
G   Skyway and stone heads
H   Plazas
I   Skyway

L1   Chapel of St. Paul
L2   Tower Theater
L3   State Capitols
L4   Central High School
L5   Ryan Hotel
L6   New York Life Building
L7   Jewell Hotel
L8   St. Paul City Hall and Ramsey
     County Courthouse & Ramsey
     County Jail
L9   Globe Building

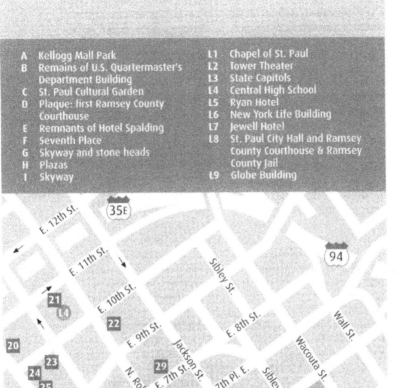

with a V-shaped central mast. His design touched off heated debate. One critic likened it to "Madonna's bra"; others rightly praised it as a dazzling work. In the end, cost concerns doomed the design, and the city settled for a far more modest concrete girder span. Although lacking the drama of Carpenter's V-mast, the bridge has some elegant touches. It may be most impressive from below, where it reveals its split structure: there's open space between the long box girders that support the north- and southbound traffic decks. The bridge also has overlooks, extra-wide sidewalks, custom-designed railings and lights, pylons with flags, and an elaborate staircase that leads down to Raspberry Island. Unfortunately, some of the ornamental work—most notably the obtrusive metal cages around the overlooks—is far too busy for the otherwise minimalist structure.

Raspberry Island and West Side Flats.

See under chapter 5.

2 Union Pacific (Chicago Great Western) Lift Bridge

Across the Mississippi River near Robert St.

L. C. Fritch and C. Chandler, with Waddell and Harrington, 1913 / 1925

One of just three lift bridges along the entire course of the Mississippi, this aging structure

blocks upstream views of the far more handsome Robert Street Bridge and is so creaky that trains have to creep across it. The little cabin atop the lift span is still manned by a bridge tender.

3 Robert Street Bridge N

Across Mississippi River between downtown and the West Side

Toltz, King and Day, 1926 / renovated and restored, TKDA, 1989

The first bridge here, an iron-truss structure, opened in 1886 and served until the early 1920s, when a higher bridge was required to accommodate a raised railroad platform at St. Paul Union Depot. Designed by Toltz, King and Day of St. Paul, the bridge is one of the most unusual in the Twin Cities. It's of a type known as a "half-through arch" or a "rainbow arch," so named because the concrete arches of the main span rise above the roadway like, well, a pair of beige rainbows. This form was dictated by the demands of the site: the bridge's roadway needed to reach Kellogg Mall at grade but also had to clear the elevated tracks of the adjacent lift bridge and be high enough to permit the passage of riverboats.

The bridge is notable as an early local example of art deco design. Although hardly a full-flowered exercise in the style, its piers and other details have a definite deco flavor. The bridge

Union Pacific Lift Bridge (left) and Robert Street Bridge

was rebuilt in 1989 by the same firm, now known as TKDA, that had designed it 65 years earlier.

POI B Remains of U.S. Quartermaster's Department Building

Beneath Kellogg Mall near Robert St.

George Wirth, 1884

Buried here are the foundation walls and ground floor of the old U.S. Quartermaster's Building, which was located near the river at Second and Robert Sts. The building, which helped supply the armies that battled Native Americans on the northern plains, was vacated and largely destroyed in the late 1920s when work began on Kellogg Mall. Its stone walls were uncovered, documented, and then reburied during the 1989 bridge reconstruction.

POI C St. Paul Cultural Garden

Southeast corner of Kellogg Blvd. and Robert St.

Cliff Garten, Ta-coumba Aiken, Armando Gutiérrez, and Xiaowei Ma (artists), 1994

A small park designed to showcase St. Paul's cultural diversity. It's serene, green, and inviting—all welcome qualities downtown.

4 Crowne Plaza Riverfront (Hilton) Hotel

11 Kellogg Blvd. East

William Tabler, 1966 / addition, Winsor/Faricy Architects, 1996

Built by the Hilton chain, this hotel sports the city's first glass-walled elevator and for many years featured a top-floor restaurant with revolving seats known, naturally, as the Carousel. Originally the hotel also offered an outdoor swimming pool perched on a second-floor plaza above Wabasha St. It was a marvelous idea for Miami but hardly practical in decidedly untropical St. Paul. Common sense prevailed, and the pool was later enclosed.

Commerce Building

5 Commerce (Chamber of Commerce) Building

2–16 East Fourth St.

Hermann Kretz, 1912 / renovated, Collaborative Design Group, 2008

Though the Commerce is not the handsomest office building you'll ever see, its second-floor windows are rare surviving examples in downtown St. Paul of the so-called Chicago window, which consists of a plate-glass center section with double-hung windows to either side. Designed to maximize light, the Chicago window was used extensively by the practical-minded architects of that city's early skyscrapers. After years of low occupancy, the building was converted into 100 units of affordable housing in 2008–9.

Oldest bridge in downtown skyway system

6 Downtown Skyway System

About 50 bridges, connecting more than 30 blocks

HGA (standard design), 1967 and later

Look along Fourth and Wabasha Sts., and you'll see at least ten of the 50 or so bridges that make up St. Paul's downtown skyway system. The first bridge (between the Pioneer Building and the Burger Federal Building) opened in 1967. From the start the system differed in two key respects from the one in Minneapolis.

Almost all of St. Paul's bridges look alike—the standard bridge is a steel truss painted dark brown and infilled with glass—whereas Minneapolis's come in an array of styles. This minimalist style echoes that of Chicago architect Ludwig Mies van der Rohe; Hammel Green and Abrahamson (now HGA), the firm that designed the prototype St. Paul skyway bridge, was an outpost of Miesian Modernism in the 1960s. Not everyone likes this uniform design, but its neutrality means that the standard bridge can be punched into almost any kind of building without creating too much architectural discord. St. Paul also differs from Minneapolis in that its skyway system is publicly maintained, much as streets would be, making for relatively consistent hours of operation from one end to the other.

It's also an unfortunate truth that St. Paul has suffered more from the negative impact of skyways than has its larger twin. In Minneapolis, the Nicollet Mall provides an outdoor pedestrian spine through the heart of downtown, and the emergence of the old warehouse district as an entertainment venue has also brought people back to the sidewalks. Downtown St. Paul, however, has become almost completely internalized because of the reliance on skyways and the web of building corridors that connect them. The streets, meanwhile, have largely gone dead. Although city design guidelines call for resuscitating street life, it's hard to see how this could happen without a reworking of the entire skyway system and its relationship to the world outside.

7 City Hall Annex (Lowry Medical Building)

15–27 West Fourth St.

Clarence H. Johnston, 1932

Standard commercial art deco, built as an addition to the Lowry Medical Building but later taken over by the City of St. Paul for offices. The interior highlight is a sleek, curving staircase that leads down from the second floor to the Fourth St. entrance.

8 Lowry Square Apartments (Lowry Hotel)

345 North Wabasha St.

*Lambert Bassindale, 1927 / addition, Ellerbe Architects, 1930 / includes **ballroom**, Werner Wittkamp, ca. 1935 / Art: relief sculptures, John B. Garatti, 1930*

Once one of the city's most prominent hotels, this straightforward brick building was converted to low-income apartments in the 1970s, when the ground floor was remodeled in a particularly hideous way. A plan to renovate the building into a mix of retail space and upscale condominiums seems to have stalled. To the north of the main building on Wabasha St. is an addition that once housed the Lowry Lounge, an art deco ballroom. A relief panel on the lounge building depicts two thinly clad Greek gods, Bacchus and Persephone, who are playing music and seem to be having a wonderful time of it.

9 St. Paul (Germania Bank) Building N *L*

6 West Fifth St. (at Wabasha St.)

J. Walter Stevens, 1889 / renovated, Wold Architects, 1989

Often overlooked even by locals, this building showcases the deep-toned beauty of Lake Superior sandstone. Its reddish brown stone, best seen in raking sunlight, was probably quarried in Upper Michigan or near Bayfield, WI. The stone is easily carved, as evidenced by the fanciful ornament that decorates much of the eight-story office building. Note

St. Paul Building

especially the intricately carved column capitals and the rich patternwork on the upper floors.

The building originally housed Germania Bank, which staged an architectural competition in 1888 and awarded the project to J. Walter Stevens of St. Paul. At least some of the design work is reputed to have been done by Harvey Ellis, an itinerant draftsman famed for his romantic renderings. Ellis did indeed work for Stevens for a time, but there's no real evidence that he had a hand in this project. Inside, the building has been modernized: the original second-floor banking hall, said to be a splendid room with deep coffered ceilings, is long gone.

POI D Plaque

Near 344 North Wabasha St. on ground floor of Victory Parking Ramp

This seldom-noticed plaque commemorates the **First Ramsey County Courthouse,** a small Greek Revival–style building that stood on this block from 1852 until 1884, when it was replaced by a much larger combined city hall–courthouse building.

10 Ecolab Building (Northern States Power Co.)

360 North Wabasha St.

Ellerbe Architects, 1932 / Art: Light, Heat and Power (bronze relief over main entrance), John B. Garatti

The old Northern States Power Company initially envisioned a skyscraper here, but the Depression intervened and only six stories were built. The building is faced in a favorite combination of the period—Mankato-Kasota stone over a base of Rainbow granite. Above the main entrance is a relief sculpture extolling the wonders of electricity. Inside, portions remain of the original art deco lobby.

Ecolab Center and Plaza

11 Ecolab Center (Osborn Building) and Plaza

370 North Wabasha St.

Bergstedt Wahlberg and Wold, 1968 / Art: Skygate (stainless-steel sculpture in front plaza), R. M. Fischer, 2000 / Above, Above (welded steel sculpture in rear plaza), Alexander Liberman, 1972

The best skyscraper of its era in St. Paul, a cut above its drab peers by virtue of its quality materials and elegant proportions. The sleek materials—polished black gabbro stone, stainless steel, and glass—project an image of cleanliness in keeping with Ecolab's business as a supplier of sanitation products and services. Situated on a templelike podium above the downward slope of Fifth St., the building is in the classic modern manner of Chicago architect Mies van der Rohe. Inside, the two-story-high, glass-enclosed lobby may well be the purest Miesian space in the Twin Cities. On the upper floors was once a penthouse apartment occupied by former CEO E. B. Osborn.

The rebuilt plaza in front of the building isn't much to look at, although a large abstract sculpture, *Skygate,* caused quite a controversy when its supposedly stainless steel began to rust soon after installation. Behind the building, above Cedar St., a far superior but largely unknown plaza features sinuous black stone benches and Alexander Liberman's colorful abstract sculpture, a perfect foil to the resolutely rectilinear building.

Macy's Department Store

12 Macy's (Dayton's) Department Store

Sixth and Wabasha Sts.

Victor Gruen and Associates, 1963

The Macy's building is an uninspired work by the Austrian-born designer best known as the architect of Southdale, the nation's first modern enclosed shopping mall, completed in 1956 in suburban Edina. When this brick box emerged from the rubble of downtown renewal, it was hailed by the local press as a signal work of modern design. Today, it's hard to fathom why. Sealed off from the city by windowless walls that enclose a parking ramp, the store has no urban presence. It also manages to commit the ultimate sin in retail architecture: it's flat-out dull.

13 Wells Fargo Place (Minnesota World Trade Center)

Wabasha St. and Seventh Pl.

WZMH Group with Winsor/Faricy Architects, 1987

Skyscrapers wearing funny hats were all the rage in the 1980s. This building's V-shaped glass top is certainly distinctive, resembling a giant cobra poised to strike at the heart of the city. Overall, however, its architecture is far more conventional than dangerously *avant-garde.* The building was originally home to the Minnesota World Trade Center, intended to become a vibrant hub of internationalism in St. Paul. The idea never took off, however, and today the building functions as a standard office tower. An indoor

Wells Fargo Place

theaters once located near the inter-section of Seventh and Wabasha Sts. Designed by Toltz, King and Day (architects of the nearby Hamm Building), the theater had an ele-gant brick and terra-cotta facade topped by—you guessed it—a tower.

14 Minnesota Children's Museum !

10 West Seventh St. (at Wabasha St.)

James/Snow Architects with Architectural Alliance, 1995

The finest of St. Paul's modern museum buildings and an object lesson in how to fit a new build-ing into a historic environment without succumbing to architec-tural nostalgia. Architects Julie Snow and Vincent James, who parted ways after this project, are best known for rigorous essays in modernism, but here they let down their collective hair a bit and produced a building that shows architecture need not be solemn to be first-rate.

shopping mall, complete with a geyserlike fountain that erupted at regular intervals, was included in the project. The mall, too, failed and has largely been converted to office space.

With its colorful brick, stucco, metal, and glass exterior, port-hole windows, and vaguely boat-like shape, the building floats like a jolly pirate ship in downtown's sea of sober gray, brown, and beige buildings. Yet its volumes are so carefully modulated that the museum doesn't seem at all obtrusive, perfectly playing off against historic neighbors like the Orpheum Theater and the Coney Island buildings. Despite a tight site, the museum also in-cludes a lovely little garden along St. Peter St., protected by a tall

Tower Theater, ca. 1940s

LOST 2 *The* **Tower Theater** *stood at 438 North Wabasha St. from 1921 until its demolition in 1959. It was one of half a dozen or so movie*

Minnesota Children's Museum

iron fence ornamented with fanciful animal heads.

A suitably playful lobby and a series of well-designed spaces showcase the museum's knack for mounting entertaining, instructive exhibits. But if you step inside, be on the alert for gangs of roving toddlers.

15 Fitzpatrick Building (Wabasha Hotel) N

465–67 North Wabasha St.

Clarence H. Johnston (Thomas Fitzpatrick, builder), 1890

The Fitzpatrick is one of the few small Victorian-era commercial buildings left in the central core. Its pressed metal corner turret (which lost its cap years ago) and oriel windows are typical of the period. It originally housed shops, offices, and apartments. The builder, Thomas Fitzpatrick, was in the construction business; son Mark became a well-known St. Paul architect.

World Trade Center Parking Ramp

16 World Trade Center Parking Ramp

477 Cedar St.

1987 / enlarged, HGA, 1998

This colorful ramp, which neatly complements the Children's Museum across the street, is a stepchild of all those garish metal facades that were tacked onto old buildings in the 1950s to "modernize" them. It's not exquisitely tasteful, true, but no other downtown parking ramp is half as much fun.

POI E Remnants of Hotel Spalding

Wabasha St. between Seventh and Exchange Sts.

ca. 1890

A sandstone column next to the south wall of the Fitzgerald Condominiums is all that remains of the Hotel Spalding, a Richardsonian Romanesque–style building located for 80 years at the corner of Ninth (now Seventh) and Wabasha Sts.

Fitzgerald Theater

17 Fitzgerald (Shubert) Theater and Fitzgerald Condominiums (Shubert Building)

Theater, 10 East Exchange St.

Marshall and Fox (Chicago), 1910 / remodeled, ca. 1933 / remodeled and restored, Miller, Hanson, Westerbeck and Bell, 1986

Condominiums, 484–96 North Wabasha St.

Buechner and Orth, 1910 / renovated, Collaborative Design Group, 2005

Home to Garrison Keillor's *A Prairie Home Companion* radio show, this double-balconied theater (originally called the Shubert and later the World) was built as a playhouse, though it also hosted vaudeville and was later adapted to showing movies. Its severe gray neoclassical facade conveys a sense of refinement, setting it apart from the gaudier vaudeville houses of the period. The theater was supposedly the first west of Chicago to feature column-free balconies. Restored in 1986, it now serves as an intimate venue for a variety of shows and concerts in addition to Keillor's weekly extravaganza.

The attached commercial and now condominium building displays a much more ebullient classical style than the theater. Its boldly colored terra-cotta fa-

McNally Smith College of Music

cades include supersized pilasters of a kind seen nowhere else downtown.

18 McNally Smith College of Music and History Theatre (Minnesota Arts and Science Center)

30 East Tenth St.

Ellerbe Associates, 1964

17 West Exchange St.

HGA, 1980

A formal type of architectural modernism that emerged in the 1960s was frequently applied to museums, usually with lackluster results, as in this building, originally known as the Minnesota Arts and Science Center. The architectural outcome would have been much different had a far more exciting design submitted by Ralph Rapson, Minnesota's leading modernist at the time, been accepted, but Ellerbe Associates' plodding effort won out in the end. At Wabasha and Exchange Sts., a newer part of the complex—built in 1980 to provide additional exhibit space for the Science Museum of Minnesota—somehow manages to be even duller than this 1964 building.

First State Capitol, 1873

LOST 3 *This block was the site of both the first and the second state capitols. The* **first State Capitol,**

Second State Capitol, 1895

built in 1853 and expanded in the 1870s by pioneer St. Paul architect Abraham M. Radcliffe, burned down in 1881. The legislature was in session, and some lawmakers barely escaped the blaze. The **second State Capitol,** *a gawky Victorian affair with a 200-foot-high central tower designed by LeRoy Buffington, opened in 1883 but proved so inadequate that planning began just ten years later for the current capitol, completed in 1905. The second capitol was then used for storage until it was torn down in 1938.*

19 St. Paul Public Housing Agency Central Offices

555 North Wabasha St.

HGA, 2004

A vaguely historicist public building, much like a number of others constructed in this area in the early years of the new century.

20 Elmer L. Andersen Building (Minnesota Department of Human Services) and St. Paul Fire Station No. 8

Andersen Building, 540 Cedar St.

BWBR Architects with Studio Five Architects, 2005

Fire Station, 65 East Tenth St.

2006

This building is nothing exceptional, but it does inject a welcome dose of color into the generally gray architectural environs of the State Capitol.

21 Public Safety Building and Penfield Hotel and Apartments (proposed)

100 East 11th St.

Public Safety Building, *St. Paul City Architect (Francis X. Tewes), 1930 /* ***Penfield Hotel and Apartments,*** *Humphreys and Partners Architects (Dallas), 2011*

A 33-story condominium tower was proposed for this site in 2005, but the project foundered when the housing market went south. A new plan announced in late 2008 calls for two separate towers housing a 170-room luxury hotel, 208 rental apartments, and a grocery store. The project, if it does indeed materialize, will also incorporate portions of the city's former Public Safety Building, a straightforward neoclassical structure that served as headquarters for the police and fire departments for over 70 years.

LOST 4 *St. Paul's* ***first Central High School,*** *a towered Victorian Gothic pile, opened on this block in 1883 and became quite a source of controversy because its cost—an unheard-of $100,000—was twice the original estimate. It was razed in 1929 to make way for the Public Safety Building.*

Rossmor Building

22 Rossmor Building (Foot, Schulze and Co.)

500 North Robert St.

Kees and Colburn, 1916 / renovated, Collaborative Design Group, 2004

Although located a block outside the Lowertown Historic District, this industrial building would certainly be at home there by virtue of its broad proportions and massive concrete-frame construction. As many as 1,000 people once worked here in a shoe factory operated by Foot, Schulze and Co. Like many old warehouses, it was later populated by small businesses in search of cheap rent and artists seeking inexpensive studio and living space. In 2004 it was converted to condominiums.

23 The Pointe of St. Paul Condominiums

78 East Tenth St.

Miller, Hanson, Westerbeck and Bell, 1988

A vaguely postmodern apartment tower from the same architects

First Central High School, 1890

Church of St. Louis King of France

who produced Cray Plaza. The architecture isn't especially pretentious, but the building's name, with its silly extra *e*, is.

24 Church of St. Louis King of France

506 Cedar St.

Emmanuel Masqueray, 1910

This parish was founded in 1868 by St. Paul's French Catholics, who built their first church that year. A second church, located at Wabasha and Exchange Sts. (the Fitzgerald Theater site), served until the dedication of this lovely Renaissance Revival–style brick church. Architect Emmanuel Masqueray is best known for the

Church of St. Louis King of France interior

St. Paul Cathedral, but he called this church his "little gem."

Extensively renovated in the late 1990s, St. Louis has a gracious, barrel-vaulted interior, one of the city's handsomest Renais-

sance-inspired spaces. Note also the large round window with its "telephone dial" pattern, a Masqueray trademark, in the north transept. At the rear, along Tenth St., a small chapel includes a replica of the grotto of Our Lady of Lourdes. The rectory next to the church presumably was designed by Masqueray as well.

Central Presbyterian Church

25 Central Presbyterian Church N *L*

500 Cedar St.

Warren H. Hayes, 1889

Central Presbyterian, founded in 1852, built its first church here two years later and enlarged it in the 1870s. Still, it proved too small for the fast-growing membership and was replaced in 1889 by this burly brownstone church, one of the city's outstanding examples of Romanesque Revival architecture. The arched entrance—a hallmark of the style—sports an abundance of carved floral and geometric motifs. The skylit interior, somewhat modified over the years, originally followed the so-called Akron plan, with seating curved around a pulpit at one corner of the sanctuary. Central Presbyterian is one of a half dozen or so Romanesque Revival churches in the Twin Cities designed by Warren Hayes, who specialized in ecclesiastical architecture.

Central Presbyterian Church interior

In 2005 the church enjoyed the unusual experience of regaining use of a lost feature: a large south-facing window blocked since the 1960s was reopened after an office building came down to make way for an addition to the headquarters of Minnesota Public Radio.

Exchange Building

26 Exchange Building (St. Agatha's Conservatory) N *L*

26 East Exchange St.

John W. Wheeler, 1910, 1914

This building was known to generations of St. Paulites as St. Agatha's Conservatory of Music and Arts, founded by the Sisters of St. Joseph of Carondelet in 1884. Besides serving as a private academy for children of well-heeled Catholic families, it functioned as a citywide convent for nuns teaching in parishes that couldn't afford their own residential buildings.

As designed, the building contained teaching studios, an art gallery, a chapel (in the smaller section at the rear), administrative offices, and even a gift shop. The upper floors housed as many as 100 nuns during peak years. Architecturally, the building has two features found nowhere else in downtown St. Paul: a double staircase leading up from Exchange St. to the main entrance and a covered rooftop garden (now enclosed), where nuns once enjoyed summer breezes high above the temptations of the city.

St. Agatha's closed in 1962, and First Presbyterian Church purchased the building. In the late 1980s it was sold to a private developer; it now functions as office space for professionals and small businesses.

Minnesota Public Radio

27 Minnesota Public Radio

480 Cedar St.

ca. 1966 / remodeled, Leonard Parker Associates, 1980 / addition, HGA, 2005

The dark brick corner building here is a mildly postmodern makeover of an earlier structure. Its mannered fenestration (semicircular windows and the like) was unusual for downtown St. Paul at the time but seems innocuous today. The glassy addition to the north tries to add a little pizzazz to the proceedings but, like public radio itself, may be too quietly tasteful for its own good.

28 Commercial building

81 East Seventh St.

Long and Long, 1907 / renovated, 2006

One of the last small brick commercial buildings left in the central core. Scores of such structures once made up the heart of downtown.

29 Alary's Bar (Elvgren Paint Co.)

139 East Seventh St.

1905 / remodeled, 1931

In the 1930s, the city widened this street (then known as Eighth) by extending its right-of-way to the north, a process that required lopping off the fronts of many old buildings and replacing them with new facades. Here the result was a delicate art deco front in glass and metal, done for longtime occupant Elvgren Paint Co.

Emporium Department Store, 1917

30 Metro Square Building (Emporium Department Store)

121 Seventh Pl. East

1911 / 1915 / remodeled, 1959, 1970 (Ellerbe Associates), 1987

One of two former department stores—the other the Golden Rule—that once formed the heart of downtown's shopping district. The store was originally quite a handsome building, faced in white brick and terra-cotta. In 1959 it was covered with a dreadful metal facade. After the Emporium went out of business, the store was turned into an office building and later enclosed in a new blue glass skin.

Securian Center

31 Securian Center (Minnesota Mutual Life Insurance buildings)

400 Building, 400 North Robert St.

BWBR Architects, 1981

401 Building, 401 North Robert St.

Architectural Alliance, 2000

The taller and older of these two buildings, 400 Robert, is very large, very gray, and very uninviting. It also thumbs its nose at its surroundings by standing askew from the street grid and presenting nothing except a series of blank walls and tinted glass at street level. It may just be downtown's least urbane skyscraper.

Across the street, the company did considerably better with a second building, completed in 2000. Instead of presenting itself as a monolith, 401 Robert offers a variety of forms and, compared to its hulking predecessor, is much more attentive to what goes on at street level. The best part is a section along Sixth St. that uses double-storied, deeply inset windows to convey a sense of heft and volume reminiscent of the old Lowertown warehouses just down the street.

LOST 5 *400 Robert occupies the site of what many people consider to be downtown St. Paul's greatest lost building: the **Ryan Hotel,** a*

Victorian Gothic extravaganza designed by Chicago architect James J. Egan that opened in 1885. It was named after its original owner,

City Center Hotel

Dennis Ryan, who made a fortune mining gold and silver in Utah before relocating to St. Paul. The seven-story, 335-room hotel, which would have made a magnificent apartment building had it been restored, was demolished in 1962, the same year Minneapolis lost its equally beloved Metropolitan Building.

Golden Rule Building

32 Golden Rule (Department Store) Building

85 Seventh Pl. East

Clarence H. Johnston, 1915 (incorporated older buildings on site) / renovated, BWBR Architects, 1985

The Golden Rule Department Store was founded in 1886 and quickly grew into one of St. Paul's largest retailers, occupying a jumble of buildings until archi-tect Clarence Johnston finally wrapped everything together under one roof in 1915. The sturdy Classical Revival–style building is quite plain except for an ornate cornice guarded by eagles posted at regular intervals. The store became Donaldson's Golden Rule and finally Carson Pirie Scott before being con-verted to office use in the 1980s.

POI F Seventh Place

Between Minnesota and Sibley Sts.

This remnant used to be part of downtown's chief east-west ar-tery, Seventh St. Movie theaters, department stores, and shops once lined this now lifeless street, which was marooned by the building of such superblocks as Town Square. As Seventh was cut into increasingly useless pieces, traffic was funneled a block north to old Eighth St., which, in keep-ing with the city's unique talent for creating confusion on the roads, was promptly renamed Seventh. Much of old Seventh (now Seventh Pl.) has been va-cated, malled, or turned into a glorified parking lot.

33 Town Square

UBS Plaza, 444 Cedar St.

SOM (Chicago), 1980

Bremer Tower, 445 Minnesota St.

SOM, 1980

Town Square Shopping Center and Park, 445 Minnesota St.

SOM, 1980

City Center Hotel, 411 Min-nesota St.

BWBR Architects, 1980

Maybe not the worst piece of architecture in downtown St. Paul, but awfully close. Hailed as a downtown savior when it opened in 1980, this megablock complex includes a largely moribund indoor shopping mall, two office towers, a hotel, and a glass-roofed park. Like its equally wretched cousin, City Center (1983) in Minneapolis, Town

Square is a clumsy gray hulk devoid of even the most rudimentary urban manners and sheathed in some of the most unattractive precast concrete

City Center Hotel

ever devised by misguided human ingenuity. Age has done little to improve matters, although HGA tried to animate the corpse with a colorful interior makeover in 2000.

The indoor park, now closed, was the most intriguing part of the design but never really worked as a public space. Had the park been carefully integrated with the shopping mall instead of placed one floor above it, it might have been a lively centerpiece for the entire complex. Instead, it became a hard-to-police place that provided too many opportunities for mischief amid the shrubbery.

The hotel displays another kind of design failure. It was built with a triangular metal roof that incorporated a solar heating system to provide the hotel's hot water needs. However, like pretty much everything else connected with this misbegotten complex, the system never worked.

LOST 6 *The* **New York Life Building,** *a 10-story, stepped-gable affair that was among the city's first skyscrapers, stood at the southwest corner of Sixth and Minnesota Sts. from 1889 until its demolition in 1967. A large bronze eagle that perched over the main entrance is now located at Lookout Park on*

New York Life Building, 1900

Summit Ave. Also on this block, at Fifth and Cedar Sts., was the 1900-vintage **Frederic Hotel,** *which burned down in 1961 in one of downtown's last big fires.*

Alliance Bank Center

34 Alliance Bank Center

55 East Fifth St.

Grover Dimond Associates, 1971

This office tower, originally home to a bank, offers a glassy, elegantly proportioned banking hall (vacant at last report) on the skyway level. The multiblock parking ramp to the rear, along Sixth St., is another story. An architectural atrocity in raw concrete and Cor-Ten steel, it's amazingly ugly and serves as a suitably dark monument to the worst impulses of urban renewal. The ramp bridges Cedar St., leaving an uninviting tunnel-like space below. The

Cedar St. crossing includes a skyway with shops (think of it as St. Paul's dismally inferior version of the Ponte Vecchio in Florence). In addition to its other architectural sins, the ramp blocks views of the State Capitol from Kellogg Mall. It's still hard to believe that one of downtown's finest old skyscrapers was destroyed to make way for this dreck.

LOST 7 *Among the lost buildings on the Ecolab site was the* **Jewell Hotel,** *a five-story brick structure built in about 1890 and located on Fifth St. just west of Cedar. The hotel is perhaps best remembered for the spectacular fire that destroyed it on August 13, 1950. By a quirk of fate, the blaze began in a ground-floor drinking establishment known as the Flame Bar.*

35 Bank and office building (First Federal Savings and Loan)

360 Cedar St.

Dykins and Handford, 1971

An aggressive little bank and office building. Sheathed in a Minnesota stone known as Winona Travertine, the portion in front of the glass-walled offices looks a bit like a refugee from the Maginot Line—fitting imagery for the bank once located here. Current plans call for the building to be demolished to make way for the proposed Central Corridor Light Rail Line linking downtown St. Paul and Minneapolis.

36 Pioneer Press Building (Minnesota Mutual Life Insurance Co.)

345 Cedar St.

Ellerbe Associates, 1955 / renovated, ca. 1980

When this building opened as the new home of Minnesota Mutual Life Insurance Co. (now Securian) in 1955, it was the first major office structure to be built downtown since the early 1930s. A lackluster building with a slightly Nordic cast, it features the long-

banded windows and spare utilitarian look favored by advocates of the so-called International Style of modernism. The three

Pioneer Press Building

skyways that now impale the building have not enhanced its appearance. Originally a large mosaic decorated the lobby, but it disappeared in about 1980 when the building was remodeled for general office use.

St. Paul City Hall and Ramsey County Courthouse, 1900

LOST 8 *Virtually all of this block was once taken up by the first combined* **St. Paul City Hall and Ramsey County Courthouse,** *an awkward Victorian pile completed in 1889 amid much municipal hoopla. The building was torn down in 1933 after the present city hall–courthouse opened. Much of its Mankato-Kasota stone was salvaged during demolition and can now be found on a number of area buildings. The* **first Ramsey County Jail,** *a rugged stone structure, was also located on the northeast corner of this block, from 1858 to about 1900.*

Downtown University Club

37 Downtown University Club (St. Paul Athletic Club)

340 Cedar St.

Allen H. Stem with Beaver Wade Day Associates, 1918 / additions, Ellerbe Associates, ca. 1960 and later / Art: ornamental plaster, Brioschi-Minuti Co., 1918

This building, typical of high-rise clubs built in many American cities in the early twentieth century, teetered at the brink of extinction in the 1980s after the St. Paul Athletic Club fell into debt and disbanded. Happily, it's found new life as home to the Downtown University Club, a fitness center, the College of St. Scholastica's St. Paul campus, and offices.

The complex interior includes gymnasiums, banquet and meeting rooms, restaurants, a swimming pool, and, on the upper floors, small guest rooms that in 2009 were being converted into a hotel. In keeping with standard Beaux-Arts practice, architect Allen Stem expressed these different uses on the exterior of the building by varying the size and shape of windows. The club's two-story-high lobby includes a baronial fireplace, ornate plasterwork, and unusual terra-cotta railings on the balconies.

38 Degree of Honor Building

325 Cedar St.

Bergstedt Hirsch Wahlberg and Wold, 1961

One of downtown's better modern-era office buildings, clad in white Vermont granite.

Globe Building, 1902

LOST 9 *The ten-story* **Globe Building** *stood here from 1887 until its demolition in 1959. Originally home to the long-gone* St. Paul Daily Globe *newspaper, the building was designed by E. Townsend Mix, the same architect who produced the legendary Metropolitan Building in Minneapolis.*

Minnesota Building

39 Minnesota Building N

42–48 East Fourth St.

Charles A. Hausler, 1930

Mild art deco. The delicately detailed entrances on Fourth and Cedar Sts., which include a version of the state seal in terra-cotta, are quite urbane.

First National Bank Building

40 First National Bank Building

First Farmers and Merchants Bank Building, Fourth and Robert Sts.

Jarvis Hunt (Chicago), 1916

First National Bank and First Trust Co., 332 Minnesota St.

Graham Anderson Probst and White (Chicago), 1931 / addition, Haarstick Lundgren and Associates, 1971

Although the First National Bank is no more, this complex still bears its name. The 32-story First National Bank Building was St. Paul's tallest skyscraper until the 1980s. Designed in a sedate, classically inspired version of art deco, the building lacks the jazziness usually associated with this style. However, it does offer downtown's largest sign, a ten-story-high, three-sided number 1 that flashes through the night. Inside, there was once a smashing art deco bank lobby on the second floor. The surviving ground-floor lobby isn't as spectacular, but it has some nice touches, particularly around the elevator doors. The 1971 addition to the north is the usual box-with–parking ramp. A colorful abstract sculpture by George Sugarman once hung like a swirl of metallic ribbons above the addition's entrance at Fifth and Minnesota Sts. It was taken down and removed to a building in Texas in 2008, for reasons unknown.

The Robert St. side of the complex includes the old First Farm-

ers and Merchants Bank Building, which at 16 stories was St. Paul's tallest skyscraper when it opened in 1916. Clad in glazed white brick, it's a fine example of the dignified Beaux-Arts commercial style that prevailed in the early decades of the twentieth century. Note the tall arched windows on the second floor. Behind these there was once a grand neoclassical banking hall, long since remodeled out of existence.

Stone heads from Germania Life Building

POI G Skyway and stone heads

Fourth St. between Robert and Minnesota Sts.

Look to the north here and you'll see the Twin Cities' highest skyway between the First Farmers and Merchants Bank and First National Bank buildings. It was built in 1931 to link the upper stories of the buildings. On the other side of the street, adorning part of Kellogg Square, is St. Paul's very own theater of redheads—sculpted sandstone giants rescued from the old **Germania Life (later Guardian) Building,** constructed on this site in 1889 and razed in 1970. It's not known who, if anyone, the eight heads depict, but they are delightful reminders of a time when no large building was considered complete without some sort of sculptural presence.

41 Pioneer (Press) Building ! N

336 North Robert St.

Solon Beman (Chicago), 1889 / addition (top four stories), 1909 / renovated, TKDA, 1983

Endicott Building N L

350 North Robert St. and 141 East Fourth St.

Gilbert and Taylor, 1890 / addition (142 East Fifth St.), 1910

Left to right: Empire, Endicott, and Pioneer Buildings

Empire (Manhattan) Building

360 North Robert St.

Clarence H. Johnston, 1891 / remodeled, ca. 1960 and later

This remarkable trio forms the finest ensemble of late nineteenth-century office buildings in the Twin Cities. Dominating the threesome is the Pioneer Building, which at 12 stories was the city's tallest skyscraper when it opened in 1889. Four stories were added in

Pioneer Building

1909. It was originally built for the *Pioneer Press* newspaper; a bulletin board where the latest news was once posted can still be seen at the corner of the building.

With its arched entryway surrounded by massive blocks of granite, the Pioneer Building was meant to convey a sense of power and permanence. Although its brick and stone facades offer a mix of Romanesque and Classical Revival elements, the building is in the no-nonsense tradition of Chicago skyscrapers of the period. Inside, much of the structure

bears the faux historic look of a late 1980s remodeling. However, its impressive 16-story-high "light court" remains largely intact. A pair of modified open-cage elevators (still run by operators) flanks a

Pioneer Building light court

spiral staircase that climbs to the top floor, where there's a dizzying view down into the light court. Unfortunately, the building was vacant as of 2009, and its future is in doubt.

The five-story, L-shaped Endicott Building wraps around the Pioneer Building. Designed by Cass Gilbert, it's a suave essay in the Italian Palazzo style and a very sophisticated building for its time in St. Paul. Within, you'll find a long arcade with a colorful barrel-vaulted glass ceiling, which was restored in the 1980s, although the vault is shallower than the original. The most intact portion of the interior is the Fourth St. lobby, which features fine stonework and an arcaded staircase.

The Empire Building, by Gilbert's longtime friend and sometime competitor Clarence Johnston, has suffered more than its

Plazas

neighbors from insensitive remodeling. The ground floor—originally done in a Renaissance Revival
style with rusticated stonework
and an arched entrance—received
an ugly makeover in about 1960.
However, renovation of the
building's interior began in 2006.

POI H Plazas

Block bounded by Fifth, Sixth,
Robert, and Jackson Sts.

ca. 1967 / Art: Triuni *and* Uniforge
(sculptures), Geoffrey Clarke, 1967

The interconnected plazas that
wind around and under the buildings on this block serve as a classic example of 1960s architectural
thinking, which held that open
space was essential to any up-to-
date downtown. Trouble is, the
plazas—adorned with abstract
sculptures and uncomfortable
benches—aren't at all inviting and
do nothing to enliven the streets
around them. Even so, the de-
signers deserve credit for one
thing: a staircase linking the
plazas to the skyway system,
where the city's real street life
takes place.

42 375 Jackson

375 Jackson St.

*Bergstedt Wahlberg and Wold,
1967 / addition (at Fifth and
Robert Sts.), Winsor/Faricy
Architects, 1980*

With its marble frame, the older
and more interesting of these
two buildings is a good example

of the formalism that was fashionable in the 1960s.

POI I Skyway

Across Fourth St. between Robert
and Jackson Sts.

HGA, 1967

This bridge connecting the Burger
Courts Building to the Pioneer-
Endicott complex was the first
link in the city's downtown skyway system and served as the
model for virtually all of the
bridges that followed.

43 Warren E. Burger Federal Courts Building

316 North Robert St.

*Walter Butler Co. with Haarstick
Lundgren and Associates, 1969 /
renovated, ca. 2006*

The federal government built this
marble-clad box in 1966 to replace
its old courts building (now Landmark Center). About the best that
can be said for it is that it's not
as bad as Minneapolis's federal
courthouse of the same period.

44 Kellogg Square Apartments

111 Kellogg Blvd. East

Convention Center Architects, 1972

A drab tower from the 1970s,
which was not a golden age in
American architecture. What little
visual interest there is comes pri-
marily from shadows cast by the
cantilevered balconies on the
tower's narrow riverfront side.

Ramsey County Government Center East

45 Ramsey County Government Center East (Farwell, Ozmun and Kirk Co.)

150–60 Kellogg Blvd. East

Louis Lockwood, 1905 / remodeled, Winsor/Faricy Architects, 1992–95

This strapping brick warehouse, built for the wholesaler behind the OK Hardware chain, is one of the Twin Cities' earliest examples of concrete-frame construction—a new structural technology that transformed American industrial architecture in the early twentieth century. The faux classical features pasted on the building during remodeling seem as inappropriate as lace frills on a football uniform.

46 Paul and Sheila Wellstone Elementary School (YWCA)

65 Kellogg Blvd. East

ca. 1910 / renovated and enlarged, Grover Dimond Associates, 1961 / renovated, 1988

A little-noticed building with intriguing modernist details. Its structural bones date to the early twentieth century, when it was a food processing plant. In 1961 it was rebuilt to serve as the downtown branch of the St. Paul YWCA.

Paul and Sheila Wellstone Elementary School

The 1960s work includes a handsome brick screen around the base of the building, an elevated entry porch, and a folded concrete roof with unusual abstract ornament beneath the folds. The building was remodeled once again in the 1980s, and it's now a public school.

Rice Park and Environs

This part of downtown was platted in 1849 by John Irvine and Henry Rice, pioneer businessmen and civic leaders (Rice later served as Minnesota's first U.S. senator). Like almost everyone else in the city's early days, the two men speculated extensively in real estate. They also seem to have been mischief-makers at heart given the peculiarities of their plat, which added a distinctive if troublesome twist to the city's street system. In an apparent effort to follow the line of the river bluffs, Rice and Irvine laid out their modified grid at a 45-degree angle to that of St. Paul Proper's 1847 plat to the east, thereby creating the decisive turn that occurs at St. Peter Street. This turn—one of the sharpest in any American gridiron city—produced an intriguing arrangement of streets, most notably the tangle at Seven Corners.

Over the years, many of these enchanting irregularities have been eliminated by street widenings, highway construction, and the development of such multiblock projects as RiverCentre (1998) and the Travelers Companies complex (1991). As a result, the Rice Park area, despite its reputation as a haven for historic architecture, is actually the least historic section of downtown in terms of its street pattern.

The area's architectural character has also changed markedly over time. Today, Rice Park and neighboring Landmark Plaza are at the heart of St. Paul's cultural life and provide an elegant setting for some of the city's finest buildings. It was not always so. Small houses and commercial buildings of varying quality ringed the park through much of the nineteenth century. The original St. Paul City Hall (1854) was the only public building facing the park until 1892, when the south portion of the Federal Building (now Landmark Center) opened. Then, between 1900 and 1920, several significant new buildings appeared on or near the park, including the first St. Paul Auditorium (1907), the St. Paul Hotel (1910), the Wilder Charities Building (1913), the Minnesota Club (1915), the Hamm Building (1920), and, most notably, the St. Paul Central Library and Hill Reference Library (1917).

Even with this handsome array of buildings, Rice Park wasn't quite the picture-postcard place it is today. As late as the 1950s, the park's architectural ensemble included, among other incongruities, an auto service garage on a portion of the site where the Ordway Center for the Performing Arts now stands. Not until the late 1970s restoration of Landmark Center and the 1985 opening of the Ordway did the park cement its iconic status as downtown's visual and cultural centerpiece.

Unfortunately, much of the area between the park and Seven Corners to the west has not been treated as kindly by time. This precinct was once home to a haphazard assortment of commercial, industrial, and residential buildings that formed a classic example of what is today the holy grail of urban planners—a genuine mixed-use neighborhood. Although the area began to decline as early as the 1950s, the period of greatest devastation occurred in the 1960s, when entire blocks were cleared for the construction of Interstates 35E and 94. So complete was this work of urban rearrangement that few old buildings survived and entire streets such as Auditorium vanished.

The completion of Xcel Energy Center in 2000 and the return of professional hockey to the Twin Cities injected new life into the Seven Corners area, where a strip of small shops, restaurants, and taverns has become downtown's most vibrant commercial corridor (though technically part of the West Seventh neighborhood; see pages 93–102). Still, the area east and north of the arena remains an urban void devoted to parking lots and fast one-way streets. One day, perhaps, it will become what it should be—a vital part of the city.

Rice Park

POI A Rice Park !

Bounded by Fourth, Fifth, Market, and Washington Sts.

1849 / plaza and fountain, HGA, 1965 / modified, ca. 2002 / Art: The Source (statue), Alonzo Hauser, 1965 / F. Scott Fitzgerald (bronze statue), Michael Price, 1996

This pleasant and urbane little park, with its distinctive trapezoidal shape, was—along with Irvine and Smith Parks—one of three public squares created in 1849 by early city developers. It was an informal place in the beginning. Local women sometimes hung their laundry out to dry while grazing animals trimmed the grass. There was also a public market here for a time, from which Market St. derives its name.

Development of the park began in 1872 when the city installed a fountain (cost: $964) and a wooden bandstand. In 1883 further improvements were made, including installation of the city's first electric street lights, in advance of a mammoth celebration marking completion of the Northern Pacific Railroad's line to the West Coast. Chester A. Arthur was among the celebrants and became the first of several U.S. presidents to orate here. In 1898 the park was upgraded again with new walkways, benches, and plantings. Except for removal of the fountain in 1925, the park changed little over the next half century.

In 1965 Rice Park took on a new look. The circular plaza and fountain that now dominate the park were installed, as was Alonzo Hauser's fetching statue. The plaza has always seemed a bit too big for such a small park, although as originally built it was broken up into a series of concentric rings created by steps leading down to the fountain. This feature was eliminated in a 2002 remodeling, and the plaza now seems larger than ever. Still, the plaza and fountain work well enough as a gathering place, and on summer afternoons the park is crowded with brown baggers eating lunch and soaking up the sun. The park's best season may be winter, when holiday lights twinkle in the trees and winter carnival ice sculptures gleam in the cold light. It is indeed an enchanting environment, and St. Paulites should count their urban blessings because few other U.S. cities can boast of a finer public square.

1 Landmark Center (U.S. Post Office and Federal Courts Building) ! N L

75 West Fifth St.

Supervising architect of the U.S. Treasury (Willoughby J. Edbrooke and others), 1892–1902 / renovated and restored, Brooks Cavin, Stahl/Bennett, Winsor/Faricy Architects, 1972–78

St. Paul's very own castle, with a fairy tale of a story behind it. Declared surplus property by the federal government in 1969, the building was a week away from

Rice Park and Environs

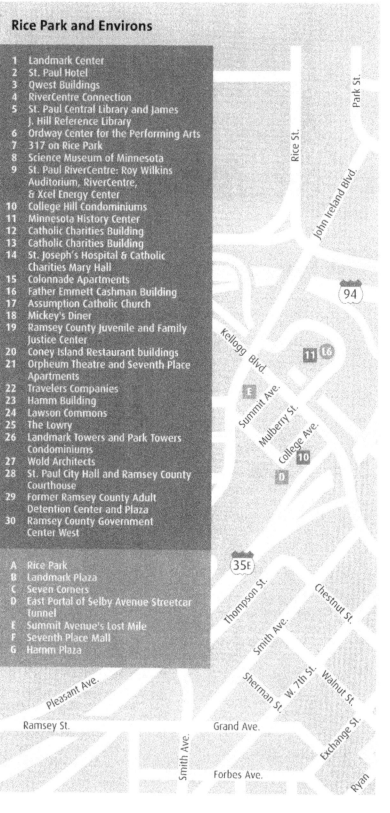

1 Landmark Center
2 St. Paul Hotel
3 Qwest Buildings
4 RiverCentre Connection
5 St. Paul Central Library and James J. Hill Reference Library
6 Ordway Center for the Performing Arts
7 317 on Rice Park
8 Science Museum of Minnesota
9 St. Paul RiverCentre: Roy Wilkins Auditorium, RiverCentre, & Xcel Energy Center
10 College Hill Condominiums
11 Minnesota History Center
12 Catholic Charities Building
13 Catholic Charities Building
14 St. Joseph's Hospital & Catholic Charities Mary Hall
15 Colonnade Apartments
16 Father Emmett Cashman Building
17 Assumption Catholic Church
18 Mickey's Diner
19 Ramsey County Juvenile and Family Justice Center
20 Coney Island Restaurant buildings
21 Orpheum Theatre and Seventh Place Apartments
22 Travelers Companies
23 Hamm Building
24 Lawson Commons
25 The Lowry
26 Landmark Towers and Park Towers Condominiums
27 Wold Architects
28 St. Paul City Hall and Ramsey County Courthouse
29 Former Ramsey County Adult Detention Center and Plaza
30 Ramsey County Government Center West

A Rice Park
B Landmark Plaza
C Seven Corners
D East Portal of Selby Avenue Streetcar Tunnel
E Summit Avenue's Lost Mile
F Seventh Place Mall
G Hamm Plaza

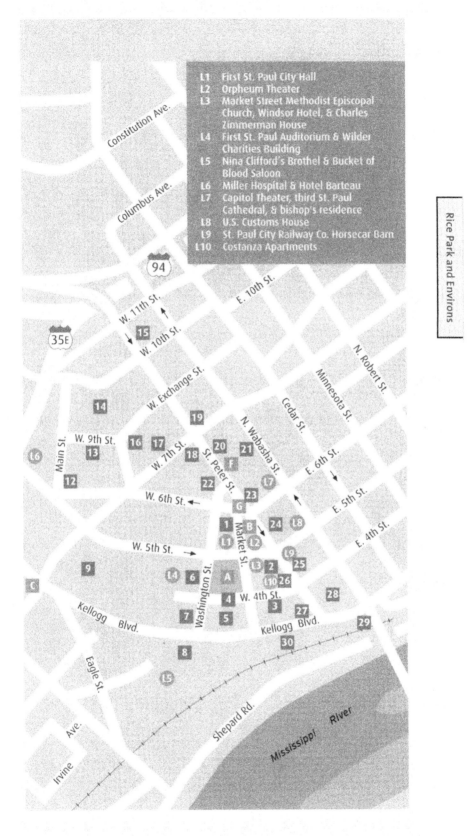

L1   First St. Paul City Hall
L2   Orpheum Theater
L3   Market Street Methodist Episcopal
      Church, Windsor Hotel, & Charles
      Zimmerman House
L4   First St. Paul Auditorium & Wilder
      Charities Building
L5   Nina Clifford's Brothel & Bucket of
      Blood Saloon
L6   Miller Hospital & Hotel Barteau
L7   Capitol Theater, third St. Paul
      Cathedral, & bishop's residence
L8   U.S. Customs House
L9   St. Paul City Railway Co. Horsecar Barn
L10   Costanza Apartments

Rice Park and Environs

Landmark Center

Landmark Center interior

possible demolition when it was saved by a coalition of city and county government officials, civic leaders, and private citizens, led by the redoubtable Betty Musser. Next came six years of painstaking restoration and renovation as the building was fitted out for its new life as home to arts and cultural organizations. Its rebirth as Landmark Center in 1978 was the first great triumph of historic preservation in St. Paul and did more than any other project to demonstrate the value of the city's architectural heritage.

The building is well worth the extraordinary effort that went into saving it. Constructed in two stages—the southern part, with a tower overlooking Rice Park,

came first, followed several years later by the northern section and its even more massive tower—Landmark Center is one of a number of magnificent Romanesque-Chateauesque–style courthouses and post offices built by the federal government in the 1890s. Similar such buildings went up in Washington, DC, Milwaukee, and Omaha, but Landmark Center may be the best of them all.

It's also a remarkably appealing work of public architecture, with none of the rather oppressive heaviness of Minneapolis City Hall (1889–1906), a contemporaneous exercise in the Romanesque Revival style. Instead of that building's raw display of civic power, Landmark Center offers a cheery array of tourelles, arcades, and gables, all rendered in smooth blocks of St. Cloud granite. The result is pure architectural romance—not a quality usually associated with federal buildings.

Within, the building is organized around a large skylit atrium, the Elizabeth Willett Musser Cortile. Offices and four old courtrooms ring this six-story-high space, one of the most dramatic in St. Paul. Don't miss seeing the third- and fourth-floor courtrooms, which display Victorian design at its most exuberant. Perhaps the finest is the fourth-floor

Sanborn Room, which showcases carved white Vermont marble beneath a stained-glass skylight. The courtrooms also have a rich history that includes the trials of notorious gangsters like Alvin "Creepy" Karpis in the 1930s.

First St. Paul City Hall, 1890

LOST 1 *The **first St. Paul City Hall**, a simple Greek Revival–style building, occupied the southern part of this block from 1854 to 1890, when it was razed to make way for what is now Landmark Center.*

POI B Landmark Plaza

Bounded by Fifth, Sixth, Market, and St. Peter Sts.

SRF Consulting Group, 2003 / Art: Peanuts Characters (three bronze statues), TivoliToo Design Studios, 2003

Charles Schulz (1922–2000), creator of the classic *Peanuts* comic strip, was raised in St. Paul. His work is memorialized by three bronze sculptures scattered about this little wedge of a park, which is finished in fieldstone, granite, and brick. The sculptures aren't to everyone's taste, but given

the abstract solemnities of some public art, Charlie Brown and his pals don't seem all that bad in comparison. One need only look across the street at Hamm Plaza— a very proper, dignified, and virtually unusable public space—to see that too much design can be as big a problem as too little.

LOST 2 *The **Orpheum (later President) Theater**, a large vaudeville house later converted to a movie theater, stood here between 1906 and 1939, when it was demolished.*

St. Paul Hotel

2 St. Paul Hotel

350 Market St.

*Reed and Stem, 1910 / renovated, HGA, 1983 / addition **(St. Paul Grill)**, HGA, 1990*

The last of the grand old downtown hotels in the Twin Cities, financed by 3M magnate Lucius P. Ordway, who contributed $1 million to the project. Occupying an irregularly shaped block at the turn of the downtown grid, the hotel is an odd building and not just because of its angled configuration. Its rather plain base and glazed-brick middle are

Orpheum Theater, 1906

crowned by a grandiose cornice that makes the building seem top-heavy. As a result, the hotel isn't as graceful as it could have been, given its distinctive site.

The frequently remodeled hotel closed in 1979 after years of dwindling patronage. Vacant and unheated, it suffered ruinous damage before new owners renovated it in 1983. Virtually nothing remains of the original interiors, which once included a rooftop palm garden. As part of the 1983 renovation work, the hotel was reoriented toward Rice Park: its main entrance had been at Fifth and St. Peter Sts. The St. Paul Grill, a popular eating spot with a clubby atmosphere, was added to the Rice Park side in 1990.

LOST 3 *Lost buildings of note on this site include the* **Market Street Methodist Episcopal Church** *(1849–1927), the* **Windsor Hotel** *(1878–1910), and the* **Charles Zimmerman House** *(1887–1924), a townhome with Moorish-Spanish touches built for a pioneer St. Paul photographer.*

Qwest Buildings

3 Qwest Buildings

70 West Fourth St.

Clarence H. Johnston, Jr., 1937 / additions, Ellerbe Associates, 1968, 1977

A case where nothing beats the original. The oldest of these three interconnected buildings is an art deco gem constructed for the Tri-State Telephone Co. It's clad in two beautiful Minnesota stones: swirling Morton gneiss at the base and Mankato-Kasota limestone above. The building is especially stunning on autumn afternoons when raking sunlight sets the golden limestone aglow. Inside the Fourth St. entrance is a handsome lobby now used as a telephone museum. The two additions to the east of the original building add little except bulk to the proceedings; the newer of the two, an overweening purple brick monolith, is particularly unpleasant.

4 RiverCentre Connection (tunnel)

Beneath Fourth St. between St. Peter and Washington Sts.

Architectural Alliance and CNA Engineers, 2002

This tunnel, linked to the downtown skyway system, was built to provide an indoor passage between downtown hotels and RiverCentre, mainly for conventiongoers and other out-of-towners reluctant to brave the brute terrors of Minnesota winter. A tunnel was dug because a skyway link would have required impaling either the library or Landmark Center with bridges or constructing a glass and steel trestle around Rice Park, any of which would have raised a mighty stink in history-conscious St. Paul.

The tunnel, which hooks up with the main skyway system near Fourth and St. Peter Sts., includes an indoor link to the Central Library and a pair of outdoor staircases leading up to Fourth. The connection, as it's called, is a superior piece of work—handsomely designed, brightly lit, and not at all, well, tunnel-like. Still, it's by no means clear that the problem of conventiongoers facing a few minutes in the cold required $10 million–worth of solving.

5 St. Paul Central Library and James J. Hill Reference Library ! N L

80–90 West Fourth St.

Electus Litchfield, 1917 / Central Library restored and renovated, MS&R Architects, 2002

One of the city's—and the state's—great Beaux-Arts monuments. Rising behind an elegant balustrade along the southern side of Rice Park, the building projects

St. Paul Central Library (right) and James J. Hill Reference Library

St. Paul Central Library interior

an air of cultured dignity, and it's probably what most people think a library *should* look like. Yet it is very much a product of its time—an era from roughly 1895 to 1925 in which classicism (in this case, of the Northern Italian Renaissance variety) served as the dominant language of American public architecture.

The architect, East Coast blue blood Electus Litchfield, got the job because his father was an associate of James J. Hill, who bankrolled the project. Even so, Litchfield came with excellent credentials, including a stint with Carriere and Hastings, architects of one of the nation's Beaux-Arts masterpieces, the New York Public Library (1911). Litchfield's task was to design a building that would seamlessly combine two institutions—the St. Paul Central Library and the privately endowed Hill Reference Library—and he succeeded brilliantly. Arched doorways reached by staircases

at either end of the Fourth St. facade express this duality.

The building's refined exterior of pink Tennessee marble is matched by its elegant interior. The Central Library's main reading room is a high point: light pours through large arched windows while overhead hand-painted ceiling beams (some sporting Litchfield's monogram, EDL) add dashes of color. Other major rooms are equally graceful. A grand staircase winds through the building, providing fine views of the Mississippi. Much of the interior is finished in Kettle River sandstone from a quarry once owned in part by Hill himself.

Central Library was designed for a "closed" system in which books were kept in stacks and delivered to patrons on request. This arrangement proved inefficient as publicly accessible shelving came into favor. Over the years many modifications were made, including the insertion of intrusive stacks into the main reading room. The library was finally restored and renovated between 2000 and 2002. Workers repainted original ornament, converted old stacks into reading rooms, created a new entry sequence, added a mezzanine in the main reading room, and built a new children's room, which incorporates from the old children's room a puppet theater designed in the 1940s by the St. Paul architect-artist team of Magnus and Elsa Jemne. Today, the Central Library looks—and works—as well as it ever has, and it remains one of the city's most beloved buildings.

The James J. Hill Reference Library, founded and endowed by its namesake, occupies the east wing of the building. Because the Hill serves strictly as a business library, it doesn't generate

James J. Hill Reference Library interior

the traffic of Central Library and is often overlooked, which is a shame given the quality of its design.

The heart of the Hill is a superbly proportioned reading room that appears to be an exercise in the uses of the golden section. The room conveys a remarkable sense of serenity, and there is no lovelier place in the Twin Cities to spend an afternoon lost in reading or research. With its sturdy classical columns, old-fashioned book alcoves, glass-floored balconies, and long reading tables lit by shaded lamps, the room has

changed little since its opening in 1917. The only defect is a lack of natural light, lost when the original skylight was covered in the 1970s. If and when the skylight is restored, the reading room will enjoy a radiant rebirth.

6 Ordway Center for the Performing Arts !

345 Washington St.

Benjamin Thompson and Associates, 1985

Built during the height of the postmodern era, when architectural pastiches sprouted like gaudy hothouse flowers, the Ordway is refreshingly understated. Its architect, St. Paul native Benjamin Thompson, used a limited palette of traditional materials—hand-molded brick, copper, stone, and wood—to craft an enduring work. The exterior's hand-molded brick is especially fine, laid up in an unusual pattern known as Flemish double header (a variation can be seen on the St. Paul Hotel).

Ordway Center for the Performing Arts interior

Inside, Thompson created an old-fashioned opera house, with a broad lobby, a sweeping stair-

Ordway Center for the Performing Arts

case where concertgoers can see and be seen, and a large but intimate auditorium that seats 1,900 people. There's also a much smaller theater used for plays, recitals, and other performances. The Ordway's acoustics has never been as successful as its architectural design. Critics—and there are legions—contend the auditorium may be a better place to see than hear the St. Paul Chamber Orchestra, which regularly plays at the Ordway, as do touring Broadway shows.

Still, the Ordway ranks among the best of downtown St. Paul's modern-era buildings, and it's hard now to imagine what Rice Park would look like without it. The building is named in honor of Lucius P. Ordway. His granddaughter, Sally Ordway Irvine, contributed a third of its $45 million construction cost.

LOST 4 *Previous buildings at this site include the **first St. Paul Auditorium** (later known as **Stem Hall**), built in 1907 and razed in 1982, and the **Wilder Charities Building**, which stood from 1913 to about 1984.*

317 on Rice Park

7 317 on Rice Park (Minnesota Club)

317 Washington St.

Clarence H. Johnston, 1915

Built for the tony Minnesota Club (founded in 1869) but now used as offices for the Minnesota Wild hockey team, this gracious structure conveys an Edwardian sense of elegance. Today, hip young executives populate the building, but if you step inside the richly finished old clubrooms, heady with the weight and power of money, it's easy to imagine ample gentlemen in vested suits sitting

comfortably in leather chairs, cigars and brandy at hand as they pore over the *Wall Street Journal* and contemplate the state of their portfolios.

For many years, legend held that a secret tunnel, hewn from the soft sandstone that underlies much of downtown, connected the club to a brothel down the hill run by legendary St. Paul madam Nina Clifford. Alas, modern excavations have failed to uncover any evidence of this supposed passageway to sin, though it's nice to think that it's still down there somewhere, awaiting rediscovery.

Science Museum of Minnesota

8 Science Museum of Minnesota

120 Kellogg Blvd. West

*Ellerbe Becket, 2000 / includes **Science House**, Barbour LaDouceur Architects, 2003 / Art: Iguana (sculpture), Nick Swearer, 1978*

An opportunity missed. Occupying a splendid site on the bluffs above the Mississippi River, this museum ought to have shouted its presence as one of the city's most important cultural attractions. Instead, it's a curiously uneventful work of architecture, polite as a gathering of Minnesota Lutherans and not much interested in standing out from the crowd.

A smidge of visual drama occurs along Kellogg Blvd., where a wall of windows thrusts up from the main entrance. Inside, the museum offers a large if not striking lobby, the inevitable Omnitheater, and a series of galleries and education spaces. A winding staircase distributes visitors to six levels while offering views of the river; there's also an outdoor staircase on the east side of the building. Outdoor balconies provide museumgoers with a chance to enjoy the scenery on pleasant days. The multilevel layout can be confusing, in part because visitors start at the top and work their way down, but the building's biggest shortcoming is a failure of imagination.

A small river-level park called the Big Back Yard lies below the museum, and here you'll find the Science House, a funky metal-clad structure of only 1,000 square feet designed to show how a building can generate all of its own energy needs, even in Minnesota's extreme climate.

LOST 5 Nina Clifford's Brothel, *St. Paul's most famous house of ill repute, stood from 1887 to the 1930s on a now vacated stretch of Washington St. below the bluffs here. Nearby was another earthy establishment known as the* **Bucket of Blood Saloon.**

Upper Landing.

See under chapter 5.

9 St. Paul RiverCentre

Roy Wilkins Auditorium, Fifth St. west of Washington St.

St. Paul City Architect (Charles A. Bassford with Clarence Wigington), 1932 / renovated, 1986

RiverCentre, 175 Kellogg Blvd. West

HGA, 1998

Xcel Energy Center, 199 Kellogg Blvd. West

HOK Sports Facilities Group, 2000

A convention complex that, to borrow a phrase from the great Chicago architect Daniel Burn-

ham, fails to "stir the blood." It's certainly better than what it replaced—the dreary St. Paul Civic Center (1973)—but it offers little in the way of architectural excitement. The main facade along Kellogg Blvd. is especially unattractive, featuring a cheap-looking glass wall beneath a clumsy second-story projection where banquet rooms are located. This overhang—the architectural equivalent of a beer belly—throws the whole design off-kilter.

Xcel Energy Center is the most successful part of RiverCentre. Although the brick-and-glass exterior is as clunky as the rest of the complex, the arena works beautifully; home to the Minnesota Wild, it has won widespread praise as one of the nation's best venues for hockey.

The oldest part of RiverCentre is Roy Wilkins Auditorium, named after the civil rights leader who was raised in St. Paul. Built as an addition to the original municipal auditorium of 1907, the Wilkins building was largely designed by Clarence Wigington, the nation's first black municipal architect. The surviving facade (along Fifth St.) is a rather plain example of the normally exuberant art deco style.

POI C Seven Corners

Kellogg Blvd. and Seventh and Eagle Sts.

In a 1927 story called "A Short Trip Home," F. Scott Fitzgerald wrote of "a sloping mid-section of our city which lies beneath the residence quarter on the hill and the business district on the level of the river. It is a vague part of

Xcel Energy Center

Seven Corners, 1906

town, broken by its climb into triangles and odd shapes—there are names like Seven Corners—and I don't believe a dozen people could draw an accurate map of it." Although this area has changed greatly since Fitzgerald's time, it's true that even those who navigate through here every day might be hard pressed to say exactly how they do it. The original intersection brought together Third (now Kellogg Blvd.), Fourth, Seventh, Main, and Eagle Sts. Today, there are only five corners—Fourth and Main were removed from the mix due to various street realignments in the 1970s—and the intersection no longer offers the splendid sense of befuddlement it once did.

West Seventh Street.

See under chapter 5.

10 College Hill Condominiums

162–68 College Ave.

Charles A. Wallingford, 1892 / 1898

These Romanesque Revival–style buildings are the last Victorian remnants of a hilly old residential neighborhood that once extended

Erasmus Deane House, 1888

northeast along College Ave. and Mulberry St. toward what is now the State Capitol Mall. Among the prominent mansions here was the **Erasmus Deane House,** built in 1869 at 173 College Ave. and demolished in 1942. Most of the big houses were already gone by the time construction of Interstates 94 and 35E transformed the area beginning in the 1960s.

POI D East Portal of Selby Avenue Streetcar Tunnel

College Ave. near Old Kellogg Blvd.

Charles Shepley, 1907

This old tunnel's lower portal can be seen from Kellogg Blvd. just

Selby Avenue streetcar tunnel, 1910

north of Seven Corners. The reinforced concrete tunnel, one of the first of its kind built in the United States, cut the grade of Selby Hill from 16 percent down to seven percent, making it manageable for electric streetcars, which previously had required the help of a counterweight system to negotiate the steep incline. The curving, 1,500-foot-long tunnel emerged in the middle of Selby Ave. near the St. Paul Cathedral. It remained in use until the last streetcar ran on July 11, 1953; the tunnel was filled in a few years later.

POI E Summit Avenue's Lost Mile

Between Kellogg Blvd. and Old Kellogg Blvd. east of John Ireland Blvd.

Before freeways, the Minnesota History Center, and other forms of progress, Summit Ave. continued another mile or so to the east of here. Descending a long slope into downtown, Summit finally ended at today's intersection of Robert St. and Columbus Ave. Apartments and two nineteenth-century houses overlook this vestigial stretch of Summit, tantalizing reminders of the kinds of buildings that once lined what might be called Summit's lost mile.

11 Minnesota History Center

345 Kellogg Blvd. West

HGA, 1992 / Art: glass etchings, Brit Bunkley, 1993 / Charm Bracelet (inlays in rotunda floor), James Casebere, 1993 / Minnesota Profiles (stone and terra-cotta columns in plaza), Andrew Leicester, 1995

Home to the Minnesota Historical Society, the History Center is the most important state building of its time. It includes exhibit halls, a library, classrooms, an auditorium, a restaurant, two museum stores, offices, and a large amount of underground storage and work space. Although it manages this compli-

cated program quite well, the building also offers its share of disappointments.

Built largely from materials of the old order—granite, limestone, copper, and oak—it's possibly the last Twin Cities public building that might invite comparison with Beaux-Arts monuments

Minnesota History Center

such as the State Capitol. Wags dubbed the building "fortress history"; indeed, it suggests a great stone keep where the treasures of the past will be safe for the ages.

Yet the History Center seems at odds with itself, as though it can't decide whether to be classical (as in the monumental facade along John Ireland Blvd.) or picturesque (the rather odd tower that dominates the building's east side). Mixed messages also abide within. Wide corridors with vaulted oak ceilings invoke the Beaux-Arts era, but the overall layout of the L-shaped building doesn't support this grand conceit. The main entrance, for example, takes you down a hallway and into a rotunda, where you'd expect to be swept into the building via a grand staircase. Instead, the stairs are all but hidden off to the side. The biggest disappointment is the library, which should be the true heart of the building. Instead, it's a very ordinary room that does nothing to convey its importance as a central repository of the state's past.

LOST 6 *The History Center occupies the site of **Miller Hospital**, which opened in 1920, closed in the mid-1980s, and was demolished a few years later. Just down the hill was another historic building of note— the **Hotel Barteau** (later known as*

Hotel Barteau, 1890s

the **Piedmont Apartments),** *a six-story Victorian that held down the now vanished corner of Ninth St. and Smith Ave. from 1889 to 1969.*

12 Catholic Charities (Knights of Columbus) Building

215 Old Sixth St.

1926

An urbane brick building originally occupied by the Knights of Columbus. **Cretin High School** was housed in a massive brick building on this site from 1889 until about 1925, when the school moved to its current location near Cretin and Randolph Aves.

13 Catholic Charities (Junior Pioneer Association) Building

192 West Ninth St.

Mark Fitzpatrick, 1909

The last of its breed downtown: a small building with a classically colonnaded porch. Its out-of-the-way location probably saved it from the wreckers, although it has lost some original features.

14 St. Joseph's Hospital

69 West Exchange St.

*John W. Wheeler, 1922 / additions, Ellerbe Associates, HGA, and others, 1960s and later / addition (**de Paul patient tower**), HOK Architects with BWBR Architects, 2008*

Catholic Charities Mary Hall (St. Joseph's Nurses' Home)

438 Main St.

John W. Wheeler, 1926

St. Paul's oldest hospital, founded in 1853 by the Sisters of St. Joseph of Carondelet. Like most hospitals, it's become an architectural hodgepodge over the years, with various additions and deletions. The latest addition is a five-story cardiac and neurovascular center spanning Tenth St. On the west side of the hospital campus is Mary Hall, a 1920s-vintage nurses' residence now used as an emergency shelter for men. Like most institutional architecture of the period, it's far more urbane than the newer buildings around it.

Colonnade Apartments

15 Colonnade (Palazzo) Apartments

532–44 St. Peter St.

Hodgson and Stem, 1889 / renovated, ca. 1899

One of four large apartment hotels built in St. Paul in the late

St. Joseph's Hospital

1880s, this building features a two-level central arcade recessed between projecting wings. The monumental gesture was unusual for its time in St. Paul and must have made a striking impression, as it still does today. The building received a minor facelift in 1899 when balconies and small window pediments were added.

By 1955, the Colonnade (then known as the Willard) was limping along as a faded but genteel old apartment hotel when disaster struck. Fire raced through the upper floors, killing a heroic maid who'd gone up in an elevator to warn residents. After the fire, the two upper floors were amputated, none too gently, leaving the abridged four-story building visible today. The old hotel dodged another potential death blow when Interstate 94 plowed a block to its north in the 1960s.

Father Emmett Cashman Building

16 Father Emmett Cashman Building (Assumption School) N *L*

68 West Exchange St.

ca. 1861–64

This small stone building, which predates Assumption Church, is a rare downtown survivor from the Civil War era. Italianate in style, it was originally home to Assumption School.

17 Assumption Catholic Church ! N *L*

51 West Seventh St.

Eduard Riedel, 1874 / Art: clock faces and other motifs in towers, Philip Larson, 1981

St. Paul's oldest functioning church structure and a nationally significant example of the nine-

teenth-century revival style variously known as Romanesque, Lombard, or even the "Round Style" (the Smithsonian Institution [1849] in Washington, DC,

Assumption Catholic Church

is another prominent example). Built of the gray, heavily stratified Platteville limestone that underlies much of downtown, Assumption is one of those landmarks that seems to have been in the city forever, its towers poking up in old photographs that otherwise depict nothing but long-vanished buildings. Legend holds that riverboat pilots used the twin towers to guide them into St. Paul.

Assumption parish is even older than the church, dating back to 1854, when St. Paul's early German settlers, many tracing their roots to Catholic Bavaria, persuaded the diocese that they needed a church of their own. The first church was finished in 1856 but proved too small. By 1869 the parish was ready to build the present church. Dedicated in October 1874, it was promptly dubbed the "German Cathedral."

Plans for the church came directly from the Old Country via a Munich architect named Eduard Riedel (not Joseph Reidl, as some sources have it). Riedel modeled Assumption on Munich's Ludwigskirche (1844), which had twin towers and was inspired by the round-arched Romanesque architecture of the early Middle Ages. Assumption is by no means a duplicate of the Munich church. Instead, Riedel abstracted and compressed the design to create a building with an almost modern sense of austerity. Assumption's distinctive multistage towers, which reach a height of 210 feet, are particularly impressive.

Assumption Catholic Church interior

Inside, the church is more ornate, with vaulted ceilings presiding over a three-aisled basilican plan that includes the usual complement of statuary and stained glass. The wooden cross to the left of the altar is one of the church's most intriguing objects. It was dug up in 1955 by children playing on a vacant lot near the State Capitol. Detective work revealed that the cross, dating to 1871, had been discarded by a parish trustee after he'd made a copy of it. Suitably enough, the cross was resurrected on Good Friday and returned to the church in time for Easter.

18 Mickey's Diner N *L*

36 West Seventh St.

Jerry O'Mahony Co., 1937–39

St. Paul's beloved greasy spoon. Although some think Mickey's is a converted railroad car, in fact it was constructed as a diner in 1937 by the Jerry O'Mahony Co. of Bayonne, NJ, which began building lunch wagons in 1913 and later graduated to full-scale diners. Shipped to St. Paul in pieces, Mickey's was assembled on site and opened for business in 1939.

Like all diners, Mickey's was built for fast customer turnover and easy maintenance. The design obviously worked: the joint is still going strong after more than 60 years of round-the-clock use. The best time to experience Mickey's is in the wee hours of the morning, when nighthawks, seeking coffee and omelets, form a scene straight out of an Edward Hopper painting.

19 Ramsey County Juvenile and Family Justice Center

25 West Seventh St.

Wold Architects, ca. 2000

A drab public building that suffers by comparison to the lively Minnesota Children's Museum across the street.

Coney Island Restaurant buildings

20 Coney Island Restaurant buildings (Vater Rhein Hotel, Gebhard Eck Hotel and Saloon) *L*

444–48 St. Peter St.

Weisen and Fischer, 1858 / Augustus Gauger, 1884 / renovated, MacDonald and Mack Architects, ca. 2001

The smaller of these two buildings is the oldest structure surviving on its original site in either downtown St. Paul or downtown Minneapolis. It dates to 1858 and

Mickey's Diner

served as the state arsenal from 1865 to 1880. The building's age is best appreciated by looking at the walls of rubble limestone on its north side. The Coney Island Restaurant opened in 1923 but has been closed for over a decade. Nonetheless, the owners continue to insist that they will reopen it someday.

POI F Seventh Place Mall

Seventh Pl. between St. Peter and Wabasha Sts.

Sanders Associates with St. Paul Planning and Economic Development Department, 1984

This mall, announced by an arch at St. Peter St., is a remnant of historic Seventh St., whose duties have now largely been taken over by what used to be Eighth St. but is now called Seventh St. Meanwhile, Seventh St. was renamed Seventh Pl. Everyone clear on that?

Orpheum Theatre (left) and Seventh Place Apartments

21 Orpheum (New Palace) Theatre and Seventh Place Apartments (St. Francis Hotel)

17 Seventh Pl. West

Buechner and Orth, 1916 / later remodelings

The Orpheum, originally known as the New Palace, was downtown's largest theater, seating 2,300 when it opened in 1916 as a vaudeville and movie house. It was constructed as part of a complex that included the 215-room St. Francis Hotel, now apartments. The theater's auditorium once offered the usual colorful testimony to the plasterer's art, but the grand space has been dimmed by remodelings and years of deterioration. Largely vacant since 1984, the Orpheum's

future remains cloudy given the large number of old theaters already operating in the Twin Cities and the potentially high cost of restoration.

Travelers Companies

22 Travelers Companies (St. Paul Companies)

385 Washington St.

*Kohn Pedersen Fox (New York) with Architectural Alliance, 1991 / includes **St. Paul Travelers South Building**, Childs and Smith, 1961 / addition, Ellerbe Associates, 1981 / renovation, Kohn Pedersen Fox, 1992*

Downtown's most notable corporate palace, designed by St. Paul native William Pedersen during his postmodernist period for a company with deep roots in the city. The St. Paul Fire and Marine Insurance Co. (later known as the St. Paul Companies) was founded in 1853 and constructed its first building on this site in 1909. It merged with Travelers Insurance 13 years after building a new headquarters complex here.

The complex is well and expensively done in St. Cloud granite and Mankato-Kasota stone, but the pyramid-roofed tower with its rounded glass extrusion looks rather chubby—a common problem in a corporate era that demands buildings with large floorplates. The design's most intriguing feature is the metal-clad entry pavilion at Sixth St. Here you'll find a vigorous space decorated with metal strips in the geometric manner of Frank Lloyd Wright. Had the St. Paul Companies (which became St. Paul Travelers in 2004 and simply Travelers in 2007) waited another five years for a new building, it might have gotten something far live-

Hamm Building

lier from Pedersen, who cut his teeth as a modernist and never seemed at home in the post-modernist camp.

23 Hamm Building N

408 St. Peter St.

Toltz, King and Day with Roy Childs Jones, 1920 / restored, Oertel Architects and ESG Architects, 1998

An elegant office building with an unusual provenance. It began going up in 1914 on the site of the old St. Paul Cathedral and was intended to be a department store for Mannheimer Brothers, once a prominent St. Paul retailer. Construction stopped, however, after the steel frame was erected in 1915, supposedly because of wartime material shortages, though financial difficulties may have been the real reason. The metal skeleton stood like a giant abstract sculpture in the heart of downtown until 1919, when William Hamm of the St. Paul brewing family stepped forward to complete the project as an office, shop, and theater building.

The building is unique in the Twin Cities because all three of its street facades are sheathed entirely in terra-cotta. Featuring classical and Renaissance motifs, the terra-cotta was manufactured by the American Terra Cotta and Ceramics Co. of Chicago in a distinctive finish called *pulsi-*

chrome. The company was so proud of its work that it advertised the Hamm Building as "a new era in terra cotta finishes."

The building's exceptionally deep basement once included a bowling alley and recreation center that functioned as a popular gambling den in the 1920s. The bowling alley is gone, as are the building's golden canvas awnings, which used to sprout every spring but were removed after suffering wind damage. Inside, the small lobby off St. Peter St. features more terra-cotta and a ceiling vaulted with Guastavino tile.

Capitol Theater interior, 1920s

LOST 7 *The northeast corner of the Hamm Building along what is now Seventh Place Mall once contained the* **Capitol (Paramount) Theater,** *the Twin Cities' first true motion picture palace when it opened in 1920. Seating anywhere from 2,300 to 3,000 (sources disagree), the Capitol was designed by Chicago brothers George and Cornelius Rapp, who decked out its facade with a flamboyant tango of Spanish-influenced terra-cotta ornament.*

Third St. Paul Cathedral and bishop's residence, 1860

The theater was demolished in 1965, but a portion of the cavernous space it once occupied is now home to the Park Square Theater.

Before the Hamm Building appeared, its site was occupied by the **third St. Paul Cathedral** *(1858–1914), a crude but undeniably powerful stone building. More impressive architecturally was the* **bishop's residence** *next door along Sixth St. The Italian Villa–style mansion cost $15,000 and was probably St. Paul's most lavish home at the time of its completion in 1860. Like the old cathedral, it was demolished in 1914.*

POI G Hamm Plaza

Sixth and St. Peter Sts.

William Pedersen and Jackie Ferrara (artist), 1992

An object lesson in design overkill. This tiny triangle, a gift of the Hamm family, was first set aside as a public plaza in 1959. In 1968 a big concrete fountain was installed, but it vanished in 1992 when the plaza was rebuilt at great expense to serve as a suitable foreground for the new St. Paul Companies headquarters complex. Pedersen and Ferrara's "high art" design, which must have looked lovely on paper, simply doesn't work well as a public plaza.

24 Lawson Commons

380 St. Peter St.

BWBR Architects, 2000

Civic leaders considered it quite a coup when Lawson Software agreed to move its corporate headquarters from Minneapolis to a new building in downtown St. Paul. Although the deal's com-

plicated financing drew criticism, the architecture turned out just fine. Many modern buildings that try to look historic fall flat on their fake pilasters, but this one works, in part because the

Lawson Commons

St. Paul–based architects clearly had a feel for the rhythms and nuances of the older buildings nearby. The building is unmistakably modern, as the curving glass penthouse demonstrates, yet its nicely proportioned brick facades allow it to fit comfortably with the historic surroundings. The art deco–inspired parking ramp and retail building along Wabasha St. is also well done.

LOST 8 *St. Paul's first major federal building, the* **U.S. Customs House,** *stood on this block at the northwest corner of Fifth and Wabasha Sts. from 1873 until 1939, when it was razed.*

25 The Lowry (Lowry Medical Arts Building)

350 St. Peter St.

Kees and Colburn, 1912 / renovated, Collaborative Design Group, 2005

This brick office building, long home to doctors and dentists, took on new life in 2005 when 135 condominium apartments were carved out of its upper ten

The Lowry

floors. The lower floors continue to be used for retail and restaurant space. The conversion yielded surprisingly bright and spacious apartments, all with the building's original terrazzo floors intact. Outside, the building's glazed-brick exterior is fairly plain, but it does offer bursts of terra-cotta ornament, including clusters of grapes, overscaled heads, and other classically inspired motifs.

LOST 9 *The most fascinating lost building on this site was the* **St. Paul City Railway Co. Horsecar Barn,** *constructed in the 1870s and later converted — in a spectacular early example of adaptive reuse — to a department store. Unfortunately, the store failed in the early 1890s, and the unusual manure to millinery saga ended when the building was demolished.*

26 Landmark Towers and Park Towers Condominiums (Amhoist Building)

345 St. Peter St. and 59 West Fourth St.

BRW Architects, 1983 / Art: La Nuova Vita (stone fountain and sculpture), Estanislao Contreras, 1983

A modern office and condominium tower of no great distinction, unfortunately oriented so that its attached parking ramp overlooks Rice Park. The architects made a feeble effort to engage the park by dressing up the ramp's facade a bit, but to no avail. The ramp also has a long, blank, overhanging wall on Fourth that offers nothing of interest for pedestrians.

LOST 10 *One of downtown's most beautiful small buildings, the* **Costanza Apartments (later Karl Hotel),** *designed by Allen H. Stem, stood here from 1889 until its demolition in about 1980.*

Wold Architects

27 Wold Architects (Women's City Club, Jemne Building) N *L*

305 St. Peter St.

Magnus Jemne, 1931 / renovation, Wold Architects, 1999 / Art: inlaid floors and other decorative features, Elsa Jemne, 1931

Is there a lovelier small building in the Twin Cities than this jewel from the husband and wife team Magnus and Elsa Jemne? A sophisticated work that skillfully mixes the zigzag and streamlined phases of art deco, it was built for the well-heeled membership of the old Women's City Club. Later it became home to the Minnesota Museum of Art before Wold Architects bought and renovated it in 1999.

Sheathed in Mankato-Kasota stone and polished black stone that steps up around the main entrance, the building has a delicacy rarely seen in institutional architecture yet also holds down its corner site with convincing authority. The equally deft interior offers a sinuous central staircase, an auditorium decorated with gold leaf, a top-floor room — once used as a restaurant — that provides sweeping river views, and inlaid floor patterns and other decorative designs by Elsa Jemne, best known for her Depression-era murals.

St. Paul City Hall and Ramsey County Courthouse

28 St. Paul City Hall and Ramsey County Courthouse !
N *L*

15 Kellogg Blvd. West

Holabird and Root (Chicago) with Ellerbe Architects, 1932 / addition and renovation, Wold Architects and others, 1992 / Art: exterior relief sculptures, Lee Lawrie, 1931 / Vision of Peace (onyx statue), Carl Milles, 1936 / bronze elevator doors, Albert Stewart, 1931 / murals, John Norton, 1931 / etched glass mural, Christopher Cosma and Denise Amses, 1991

This remarkable public building, a masterpiece of American art deco, is the result of both brilliant design and fortuitous timing. Built at a cost of $4 million to replace the old city hall–courthouse a block away, it was financed as part of a city bond issue approved in 1928. By the time construction actually began in 1931, however, the cost of materials and labor had plunged as the Great Depression gripped the nation. Gifted with a virtually unlimited budget, the architectural team—led by Holabird and Root of Chicago—was able to specify only the finest in materials and equipment, much of it

custom-made, for the new building, which was formally dedicated in December 1932.

Stylistically, the building combines two types of art deco—the early perpendicular style, with its facets and setbacks, and the later streamlined phase, visible in its many curved interior details. Holabird and Root had already shown its mastery of art deco in the Chicago Board of Trade Building (1930), to which the city hall–courthouse bears considerable resemblance.

With its stepped-up massing, wide piers of Indiana limestone, and dark vertical window bands, the building is all business and might pass for a commercial skyscraper. In this regard, it differs from lushly ornamented art deco city halls built at about the same time in Buffalo, NY, and Kansas City, MO. Exterior ornament is largely confined to unobtrusive bas-relief sculptures around the entrances. Unfortunately, the city defaced the building's Fourth St. facade by ramming a skyway through it.

St. Paul City Hall interior

Inside, business gives way to pure architectural pleasure, beginning with the War Memorial Concourse, dedicated to Ramsey County soldiers who died in World War I. Straight out of Hollywood by way of a Gothic cathedral, the concourse features pillars of black Belgian marble inscribed with the soldiers' names, dramatic bronze light wands, a mirrored ceiling, and, as its centerpiece, a 36-foot-tall statue of an Indian leader carved out of white Mexican onyx. Originally known as the *Indian God of Peace*, the statue was politically corrected in the 1990s to become the *Vision of Peace*. To courthouse denizens, however, the big fellow will always be known as "Onyx John."

St. Paul architect Thomas Ellerbe brought in Swedish sculptor Carl Milles to design the statue, which was made by a team of local craftsmen and installed in 1936. At first glance the concourse appears to hover perilously close to kitsch, yet the statue and its dark surroundings exert a kind of hushed magic: schoolchildren on tour grow quiet and even adults find themselves whispering in the presence of the great onyx god, who rotates on his mirrored base. It's theater, but of a very powerful and moving kind.

There's much else of note in the building. The Kellogg Blvd. lobby leads to six beautifully paneled elevator cars with bronze doors by artist Albert Stewart. Another highlight is the third-floor city council chambers, a sleek room adorned with murals by Chicago artist John Norton. The room is laid out so that council members are in the center, surrounded by the public, whose business they are presumed to be doing. On the upper floors a series of richly paneled courtrooms have a similar populist feature—the witness chair, rather than the judge's bench, serves as the focal point.

Fine details abound throughout, including custom-designed bronze and glass light fixtures, 25 different types of wood (among them such exotic species as Tasmanian oak and West African amipera), and 14 varieties of stone. Hardware, signs, and furniture were designed with equal care.

In 1992 a team led by Wold Architects of St. Paul completed a $48 million renovation, restoration, and expansion of the building. Three stories that fit seamlessly with the original building were added at the corner of Fourth and St. Peter Sts., where the **Ramsey County Jail** (1903–80) once stood. The architects also created neodeco interiors, including courtrooms, offices, and a basement concourse. If you find your way to the basement, don't miss the Glass Mural Commons, which offers a narrated sound-and-light show devoted to the history of the city and county.

29 Former Ramsey County Adult Detention Center and Plaza

12–14 Kellogg Blvd. West

Wold Association and Gruzen Associates, 1980 / Art: Sky (sculpture on rooftop plaza), Georgette Sosin, 1981

Before St. Paul got serious about revitalizing its riverfront, Ramsey County erected this jail on the bluffs beneath Kellogg Blvd. The detention center, which closed in 2003, offered inmates the best river views in town through unusually large cell windows. Putting a jail on the riverfront was hardly an inspired example of urban planning, but it surely served as a perverse form of psychological punishment for offenders. Legend holds that some inmates expressed their unhappiness over this situation by "mooning" passing boaters. Although there was some talk after the jail closed of converting it into apartments or a hotel, those ideas fizzled, and the building's future remains uncertain.

30 Ramsey County Government Center West (West Publishing Co.)

50 Kellogg Blvd. West

various architects including J. Walter Stevens (1886) and Reed and Stem (1911), ca. 1886 and later / renovated (new facade), ca. 1940s / remodeled, ca. 1990s

An architectural rule of thumb: the number of banners on a building tends to be inversely proportional to its design quality.

This complex of six buildings, constructed between the 1880s and 1960s for the West Publishing Co., has many banners, part of a largely futile effort to make it look like something other than a big dull lug. West decamped to the suburbs in 1992 and donated the buildings to Ramsey County, which adapted them to governmental use. In 2004 the Minnesota Museum of American Art moved into the complex's western end but closed indefinitely in 2009. Ramsey County and the City of St. Paul have considered several proposals for redeveloping the site, which offers prime riverfront views, but so far nothing has materialized.

3 Lowertown

Lowertown

As its name indicates, Lowertown lies below the blufftop plateau occupied by the rest of downtown St. Paul. Its name also derives from its proximity to the Lower Landing on the Mississippi River at the foot of Jackson Street. This landing was the city's main docking point in steamboat days, and a commercial and warehousing district inevitably grew up around it. Geography also abetted Lowertown's growth once railroads arrived in the 1860s. Early rail lines negotiated St. Paul's hilly terrain via two natural corridors: the Mississippi River and the wide valley of Trout Brook, which enters the river at Lowertown's eastern edge. Because of its location at this critical juncture, Lowertown was perfectly positioned to become a warehousing and manufacturing district as St. Paul began its period of explosive growth in the 1880s.

In its natural state, Lowertown actually had some high ground— a hill that rose 50 feet above the present level of Mears Park. Known as Baptist Hill after a small church built atop it, this prominence was gradually carved away beginning in the 1870s to accommodate development and to provide fill for the rail lines being built though the boggy bottoms of the Trout Brook valley.

Before warehouses and manufacturing buildings spread northward from the river, much of Lowertown was occupied by housing. Some of St. Paul's largest mansions could once be found here along Eighth and Ninth streets and in the old Lafayette Park area near today's intersection of Grove Street and Lafayette Road. All of these early mansions are gone, swallowed up by commercial development and the ever-expanding railroads, which chewed away large chunks of historic Lowertown in the early twentieth century.

The historic warehouses that dominate Lowertown today represent two distinct eras of building. The older generation dates from the 1880s to about 1905 and consists of massive brick bearing-wall structures typically constructed with interior frames of iron, steel, or timber. While many of these buildings survive, others were superseded early in the twentieth century by the second generation, new "daylight" warehouses built with concrete frames that permitted large windows.

Like many another old warehouse and manufacturing district, Lowertown by the 1960s was deep into decline as businesses moved elsewhere. In the 1970s, however, artists and other intrepid urbanites began to infiltrate the district, setting up studios and residences in the old warehouses. During this time Lowertown had a rather funky air to it—a little bit of SoHo transferred to the Midwest.

More formal changes soon followed. Industrialist Norman Mears began to stir the pot in the early 1970s, but the creation of the quasi-public Lowertown Redevelopment Corp. in 1978 really spurred a transformation. The designation of the Lowertown Historic District in 1983 also was crucial. Before long, one old warehouse after another was being converted to office or housing use as part of a strategy to create an "urban village." New construction included Cray (Galtier) Plaza (1986), a huge multi-use project that proved to be a financial debacle. Recent development has focused north of East Seventh Street in the so-called Wacouta Park area, where scores of new apartments and condominiums were built in the early 2000s.

Despite its successes, Lowertown has never achieved the vibrancy of Minneapolis's warehouse district. In its cleaned-up, carefully restored state, Lowertown has always seemed slightly embalmed. This quality is evident in the district's newer buildings, which tend to be timid brick boxes. Still, Lowertown continues to grow, with new and redeveloped housing now filling in the area to the north. The key to Lowertown's future, however, lies along the riverfront—now effectively blocked by the U.S. Post Office complex (1934) and the elevated rail platform that once served the Union Depot. When new development reaches the river, as it inevitably will, Lowertown may finally burst fully to life.

Mears Park

POI A Mears (Smith) Park ! N *L*

Bounded by Fifth, Sixth, Sibley, and Wacouta Sts.

1849, 1880s, and later / rebuilt, William Sanders, 1973 / rebuilt, Brad Goldberg and Don Ganje, 1992

Quite possibly the most pleasing urban square in the Twin Cities, although it took nearly 150 years for the park to take on its current form. Originally named after Robert A. Smith, an otherwise obscure speculator who donated the site to the city in 1849, the park wasn't developed until the 1880s, after Baptist Hill had been leveled. For many years it was a standard urban square with a central fountain from which sidewalks radiated to each corner.

In 1973 the park was drastically altered, and not for the better. A new design encased much of the park in brickwork, which promptly began to crumble. The park's name was also changed at this time to honor Norman Mears. The "brickyard," as it was popularly known, reached such a state of disrepair that the park was in need of complete rebuilding by the late 1980s.

The new park, designed by Dallas artist Brad Goldberg and St. Paul Parks landscape architect Don Ganje, proved to be a local wonder. Seamlessly mixing formal and informal elements, the park—with its rushing stream, rough-cut stone benches, generous plantings, and bandstand—is the finest modern-era design of any kind in Lowertown, a most pleasant place to while away a summer afternoon doing nothing in particular.

The park also provides an ideal vantage point for appreciating Lowertown's architectural fabric. Note that the historic warehouses—despite inevitable differences in size, style, and color—work together as a group, forming a brick street wall that defines the edges of the park and gives it the feel of an outdoor room. Although the businessmen who built Lowertown were rugged individualists (none more so than James J. Hill), they shared a belief in the need to construct strong, dignified buildings and thereby ended up creating one of the most cohesive architectural ensembles in the Twin Cities.

1 Cray (Galtier) Plaza *L*

175 East Fifth St., 380 Jackson St.

*Miller, Hanson, Westerbeck and Bell, 1986 / incorporates facades (on Sibley St.) of **Bishop Block**, Asher Bassford (builder), ca. 1883, and **J. P. Allen Building**, J. Walter Stevens, 1888 / also includes **YMCA**, Miller, Hanson, Westerbeck and Bell, 1985*

When it opened as Galtier Plaza in 1986, this complex promised to be the complete downtown package,

Lowertown

1   Cray Plaza
2   Mears Park Place
3   Park Square Court
4   Konantz Saddlery Co. Building &
     Koehler and Hinrichs Co. Building
5   River Park Lofts
6   St. Paul Fire Station No. 2
7   Gilbert Building
8   East Seventh Street historic
     commercial row: Bonnie Jean
     Bungalows, Heritage House
     Apartments, Constans Block,
     & O'Connor Block
9   Walsh Building
10 Block 19 Parking Ramp
11 Produce Exchange Building
12 Embassy Suites Hotel
13 Renaissance Box
14 First Baptist Church
15 Wacouta Commons area
16 St. Mary's Catholic Church
17 Allen Building
18 Industrial Building
19 Market House Condominiums
20 Apartments
21 St. Paul Farmers' Market
22 Lowertown Commons
23 Northern Warehouse Artists'
     Cooperative
24 Tilsner Artists' Cooperative
25 Chicago Great Western Freight
     Condominiums
26 Great Northern Lofts
27 Lowertown Lofts
28 Main U.S. Post Office
29 Brooks Building
30 180 East Fifth
31 Straus Apartments
32 Sibley Square
33 Minnesota Telecenter
34 Union Depot Place
35 American House Apartments
36 262 Studios
37 Lot 270 Condominiums
38 Northwestern Building
39 Parkside Apartments
40 Mears Park Centre:
     Fairbanks-Morse Co. Building &
     Powers Dry Goods Co. Building
41 Cosmopolitan Apartments

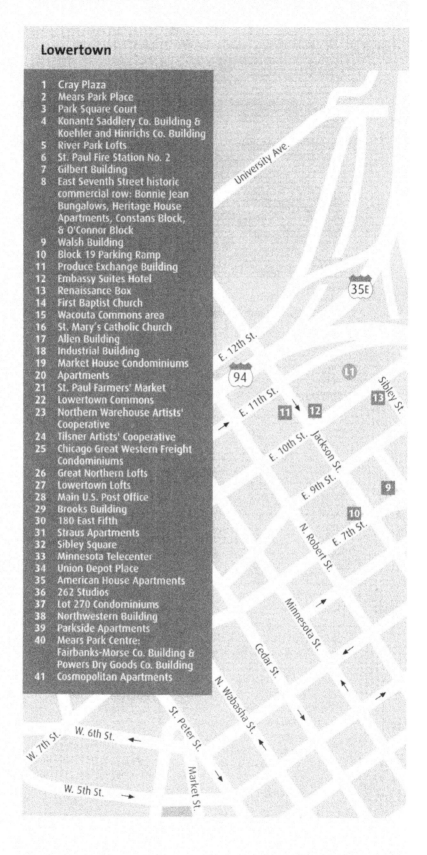

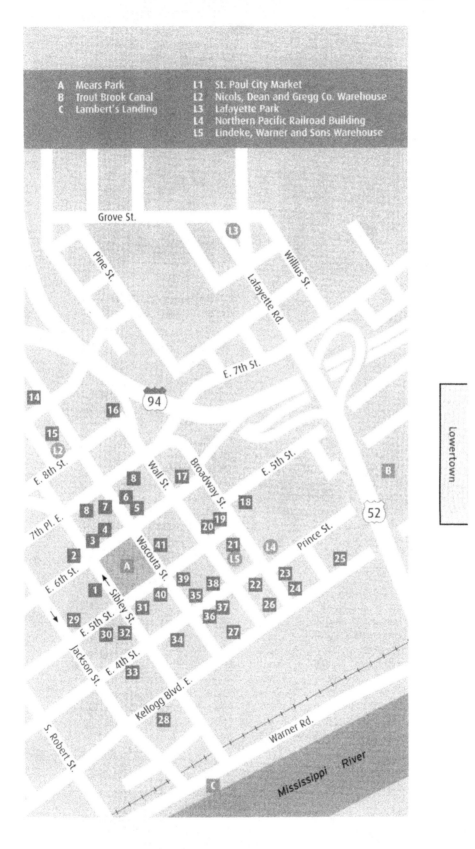

A   Mears Park
B   Trout Brook Canal
C   Lambert's Landing

L1   St. Paul City Market
L2   Nicols, Dean and Gregg Co. Warehouse
L3   Lafayette Park
L4   Northern Pacific Railroad Building
L5   Lindeke, Warner and Sons Warehouse

a dolled-up postmodern Babylon amid the sober old warehouses of Lowertown. Cray Plaza (renamed in 2009 to mark the arrival of Cray, Inc. as a major new tenant) was designed to accommodate a wide variety of uses under one large

Cray Plaza

(and, as it turned out, quite leaky) roof. Incorporating a pair of old brick building facades along Sibley St., it included two towers with condominiums and rental apartments, a new home for the downtown YMCA, and a block-long, skylit atrium with shopping on the first three levels and offices above. Elaborately finished, the shopping mall was St. Paul's version of the "festival marketplace" concept so popular in the 1980s.

It was all a grand idea, but it never worked. A chimera spun of hope and some very creative financing, the complex quickly became a sinkhole into which money and reputations drained away, until a buyer finally snapped up much of it at a fire-sale price. Today, the nicely designed apartments and condominiums have kept the place going. Meanwhile, the once colorful mall, converted largely to office use, has been painted a penitential white as if to atone for its initial excesses.

2 Mears Park Place *L*

401 Sibley St.

BWBR Architects, 1978

The layout of this apartment complex, which wraps around a large central courtyard, is nice enough, but there's way too much con-

crete. The street elevations, set behind rough concrete walls, are especially unappealing.

Park Square Court

3 Park Square Court (Noyes Brothers and Cutler Co.) N *L*

215–25 East Sixth St., 400 Sibley St.

J. Walter Stevens, 1886 / 1889 / 1906 / renovated, ca. 1971–73 / renovated, Miller, Hanson, Westerbeck and Bell, BWBR Architects, 1982 and later

This is the largest in a block-long row of buildings—all designed by architect J. Walter Stevens—that forms the north wall of Mears Park. Built for a drug and medical supply wholesaler, the complex was seamlessly expanded in 1906. Richardsonian Romanesque in style, it's among the most handsome of Lowertown's warehouses, with sweeping ground-floor arches and tight Victorian brickwork. The arches are strikingly similar to those in a Chicago warehouse designed a year or so earlier by one of that city's greatest architects, Louis Sullivan. Unfortunately, Park Square Court's original double-hung windows were replaced with inappropriate single-pane glass during a 1970s remodeling. Inside, there's a five-story atrium that dates to another renovation in 1982.

4 Konantz Saddlery Co. Building N *L*

235 East Sixth St.

J. Walter Stevens, 1893 / renovated, ca. 1980s

Koehler and Hinrichs Co. Building N *L*

237 East Sixth St.

J. Walter Stevens, 1891 / renovated, ca. 1980s

These warehouses beautifully complement the Noyes Brothers and Cutler building next door. Koehler and Hinrichs Co. was an eclectic wholesaling firm whose line of goods included "high-class bar outfits" and "fancy groceries." Today, both buildings are used for offices and shops.

5 River Park Lofts (George Sommers Co.) N *L*

245 East Sixth St.

J. Walter Stevens, 1905 / renovated, ca. 1970s / renovated, MS&R Architects, 2006

The latest of six warehouses that Stevens designed around Mears Park. The building's original occupant dealt in toys, notions, and the inelegantly described "cheap counter supplies." In the 1970s the structure was converted to office use and renamed the Lowertown Business Center after being bought by the now defunct Control Data Corp. The building has since been converted to loft-style condominiums.

6 St. Paul Fire Station No. 2 (later No. 4) N *L*

Wacouta St. between Sixth and Seventh Sts.

1921 / renovated, 2006

A small gem, long used for storage but recently renovated into apartments. Note the relief sculpture in the parapet that depicts a pair of firemen beside a plaque marking the building's construction date.

Gilbert Building

7 Gilbert Building (T. L. Blood Warehouse) N *L*

413 Wacouta St.

Cass Gilbert, 1894 / renovated, ca. 1980s

One of Gilbert's attractive warehouse buildings, this time in a Renaissance Revival mood. The building was renovated in the 1980s for office use.

8 East Seventh Street historic commercial row N *L*

South side of East Seventh St. between Sibley and Wall Sts.

Bonnie Jean Bungalows (J. H. Weed store and flats), 212 East Seventh St.

East Seventh Street historic commercial row

Lowertown

*Denslow W. Millard, 1884 / reno-
vated, 2006*

Heritage House Apartments, 218
East Seventh St.

*A. D. Hinsdale, 1882 / renovated,
ca. 1990*

Constans Block (Hotel Economy),
224–40 East Seventh St.

Augustus Gauger, 1884

Commercial blocks, 246–56 East
Seventh St.

*A. D. Hinsdale, 1882 / Omeyer and
Thori, 1889 / renovated, 2006*

O'Connor Block, 264–66 East
Seventh St.

Emil Ulrici, 1887

Although not all of these old commercial buildings have found a
sympathetic new use—part of
Butwinick's Building in the Constans Block, for example, is used
to park cars—they provide a good
sense of what much of this part
of Lowertown once looked like.
Taken together, they form one
of the last great rows of 1880s
commercial buildings in St. Paul.
They've survived in part because
when Seventh was widened in the
1930s all the rebuilding occurred
on the other side of the street. It's
instructive to compare the ornate
facades of these buildings against
the much more sparsely detailed,
albeit openly nostalgic, apartments
across the way. Of all the buildings here, the O'Connor Block,
with its two outsized dormers, is
probably the most interesting.

Walsh Building

9 Walsh Building N *L*

189–91 East Seventh St.

Edward P. Bassford, 1888

Few small Victorian buildings
have survived in downtown St.
Paul. By a stroke of good fortune,
the Walsh Building happens to
be an exceptionally nice one. Note,
for example, the intricate detail
around the arched second-floor
windows.

10 Block 19 Parking Ramp

Seventh and Jackson Sts.

Collaborative Design Group, 2004

Most of St. Paul's newer downtown parking ramps are done in
some vague semblance of historic style. Here the architects
appear to have made a stab at
art deco.

11 Produce Exchange (Bank) Building

523 Jackson St.

*1915 / renovated, Design for
Preservation and Karen Gjerstad,
2004*

An early twentieth-century brick
building, originally home to the
Produce Exchange Bank, which
served the large city market once
located across the street. In its
later years, the building languished
as second-tier office space, only
to take on a new life as loft
apartments in 2004.

12 Embassy Suites Hotel

175 East Tenth St.

Arthur Valdez and Co. Ltd., 1983

One of St. Paul's first essays in
historically reminiscent post-
modernism, though the style
being recalled here is elusive.
Inside, there's a pleasant atrium
with a pool and lots of greenery.

LOST 1 *This site was home to the*
St. Paul City Market *from 1902
to 1981. At its zenith in the 1930s
and 1940s, the market covered four
square blocks, offered 682 stalls, and
served as a regional center for the
produce trade. The* ***Produce Exchange Building*** *(now apartments)
and the* ***Eisenberg Fruit Co.*** *at Tenth
and Jackson Sts. are remnants of
the market-related businesses that
once dominated here. The market
began to languish by the 1950s and*

in its last years functioned largely as a parking lot. Despite efforts to save it, the market was torn down in 1981 and relocated to a new, smaller site in Lowertown.

13 Renaissance Box

509 Sibley St.

Butler Brothers Construction Co., 1914 / renovated, 2002

This old shoe factory was converted to commercial use in 2002, then renovated again just four years later to accommodate affordable housing units on the upper floors. A six-foot-high replica of the Statue of Liberty once adorned the roof, courtesy of the building's owner, who's half French.

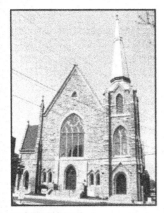

First Baptist Church

14 First Baptist Church ! N L

499 Wacouta St.

William Boyington (Chicago) with Monroe and Romaine Sheire, 1875 / additions, Milton Bergstedt, 1950s and later / new steeple, Milton Bergstedt, 1967 / Art: copper doors, Hillis Arnold, 1971

A historic limestone church built for Minnesota's oldest Baptist congregation, founded in 1847 when pioneer teacher Harriet Bishop established a Sunday school. The first church was on Baptist Hill (now Mears Park); this church—the third—was dedicated in 1875.

Architect William Boyington, whose best-known work is the old stone water tower on Michigan Ave. in Chicago that survived the great fire of 1871, produced a

straightforward Gothic Revival design here. A corner tower and a large stained-glass window above the entrance dominate the composition. The original steeple, much taller (and handsomer) than the current one, and a triple-arched entrance porch were removed in 1945: their weight threatened part of the structure built on an old creek bed.

Inside, five black walnut hammer beams rising from ornate brackets support the sanctuary's ceiling. The excellent stained-glass windows reflect the congregation's early wealth; its membership included some of St. Paul's business elite, many of whom resided nearby.

Wacouta Commons area

15 Wacouta Commons area

Area northeast of East Seventh and Sibley Sts.

***Wacouta Commons Park,** ca. 2005 / **Sibley Park Apartments,** Paul Madson and Associates and KKE Architects, 2002 / **Essex on the Park Town Homes and Apartments,** Paul Madson and Associates, 2002 / **Sibley Court Apartments,** KKE Architects, 2003 / **Dakota on the Park Town Homes and Apartments,** LHB Architects and Engineers, 2003 / **Ninth Street Lofts** (Workforce Center of St. Paul), 1909 / renovated, ESG Architects, 2004 / **Printer's Row Condominiums,** ESG Architects, 2005*

For much of the modern era, this portion of Lowertown consisted largely of old warehouse and industrial buildings interspersed with parking lots. After many fits and starts, development dollars finally started pouring into the area in the late 1990s; since then it has filled with new and renovated housing. A new green space called Wacouta Commons Park serves as the centerpiece.

The apartments, townhomes, and condominiums here are all done in the nostalgic brick mode that for a time seemed a virtual requirement for new downtown housing in St. Paul. While the buildings surrounding Wacouta Commons are decent examples of their kind, they embody the mistaken notion that buildings must look "old" to fit within historic districts. They're also much too restrained for their own good. Lowertown has long needed a jolt of architectural caffeine, but these buildings are strictly decaf.

LOST 2 *Among the lost buildings of note in this area is the* **Nicols, Dean and Gregg Co. Warehouse,** *205 East Eighth St., an exceptionally handsome 1906 brick and concrete building demolished in 1989. One of the largest mansions that stood in this vicinity was the* **Bartlett Presley House,** *at 229 East Eighth St. Built in the Greek Revival style in 1856 and later enlarged, the house—like most other Lowertown mansions—was gone by 1900.*

St. Mary's Catholic Church

16 St. Mary's Catholic Church

261 East Eighth St.

Damon O'Meara and Hills, 1921 / addition (new steeple), 2006

The wealthy Catholic businessmen who lived in Lowertown frequented the first St. Mary's Church, a long-vanished stone structure built in 1867 and located a few blocks to the east. This church is a well-kept work in the brick Gothic Revival style popular in the 1920s. It offers one

unexpected delight—a huge gargoyle who looks out, none too happily, over the freeway interchange that swallowed up much of this old neighborhood in the 1960s. The white steeple that adorns the tower is out of character with the rest of the church.

LOST 3 *Across the Interstate 94– 35E junction from the Wacouta Park neighborhood is an industrial area that was once St. Paul's mansion district, organized around* **Lafayette Park** *(a vanished square near present-day Lafayette Rd. and Grove St.). In the 1860s and 1870s, merchant princes such as James J. Hill, Amherst Wilder, Horace Thompson, and Henry Sibley built estates here, some of them encompassing an entire square block. Industrial development driven by nearby rail tracks soon made the area less desirable, however, and in the 1880s the moneyed class began to leave for, in most cases, Summit Ave. By 1920 new rail lines and freight houses had taken up much of the land south of Grove and only scattered housing remained. Today, there is none.*

17 Allen Building N *L*

287 East Sixth St.

George H. Carsley?, 1907 / addition, 1915

A six-story warehouse with unusually short, wide windows above its rusticated ground floor. It's not the handsomest building in Lowertown, but it succeeds in conveying a sense of rugged strength.

18 Industrial (Gillette Co.) Building

310 East Fifth St.

Austin Co.?, 1970 / Art: Muscle (stainless-steel sculpture), Fourth and Broadway Sts., Amy Toscani, 2004

A large manufacturing plant originally built for the Gillette Co. Its blank brick walls create a suitably plain backdrop for Amy Toscani's fanciful sculpture. The building was vacant as of 2008, but a plan is being considered to convert it into a maintenance shop for the proposed Central Corridor Light Rail Line.

Northern Pacific Railroad headquarters, 1890

LOST 4 *The site of the Gillette Co. plant was for many years the head-quarters of the* **Northern Pacific Railroad,** *which built its central offices at Broadway and Prince Sts. in 1883 and enlarged them with an elegant addition designed by Cass Gilbert in 1896. Both buildings were demolished in 1929 when the railroad constructed new tracks and a freight house on the site.*

19 Market House Condominiums (Tighe Building) N *L*

289 East Fifth St.

J. Walter Stevens, 1902 / renovated, Lilyholm Young and Gleeson, 1984

Once known as the Tighe Building and later used by the Cardozo Furniture Co., this was one of the first Lowertown warehouses to be converted into condominiums.

20 Apartments (Crane-Ordway Building) N *L*

281–87 East Fifth St.

Reed and Stem, 1904 / renovated, Cermak Rhoades Architects, 2006

Converted into over 60 units of affordable housing in 2006 after standing vacant for three decades, this chunky brick warehouse was built for the Crane and Ordway Co., which manufactured valves and fittings used for steam engines and other industrial equipment. Not long after the building was finished, company president Lucius P. Ordway secured control of another business, an up-and-coming firm known as the Minnesota Mining and Manufacturing Co. (now 3M). It did very well for him.

St. Paul Farmers' Market

21 St. Paul Farmers' Market N *L*

Fifth and Wall Sts.

Nemeth Associates, 1982 / enlarged and remodeled, Krech, O'Brien, Mueller and Wass, 2004 / **Farmers' Market Flats** *(proposed), 2010?*

The Farmers' Market is one of Lowertown's success stories and a very popular place during summer weekends, even though it's always seemed cramped on this site. A 2004 remodeling resulted in a new roof, more stalls, and a much-improved color scheme. A plan was announced in 2006 to expand the market across Wall St. into an indoor section located on the ground floor of a new 44-unit condominium building. But the project stalled amid financing controversies after construction began. Finally, the city took over, planning to build rental apartments beginning in 2010.

LOST 5 *The site of the market was occupied by the* **Lindeke, Warner and Sons Warehouse (later Toni Co.),** *which opened in 1908 and was razed in 1970.*

22 Lowertown Commons (St. Paul Rubber Co.) N *L*

300 East Fourth St.

1905 / renovated, Bower Lewis Thrower Architects (Philadelphia), 1987

Building close to the river has always posed foundation problems: the ground in parts of Lowertown is little more than casual riverfront fill. This warehouse had settled so badly on its

Lowertown Commons

southern side that it had to be substantially rebuilt before its conversion to apartments in the 1980s. Inside, there's an atrium created by tearing out walls and floors and exposing a portion of the building's structural frame.

23 Northern Warehouse Artists' Cooperative (Northern Pacific Railroad Warehouse) N *L*

308 Prince St.

Northern Pacific Railroad (in-house architect), 1908 / renovated, 1990

The largest remnant of the Northern Pacific Railroad headquarters complex that once clustered around Prince and Broadway Sts. This warehouse is historic for another reason: it was the first development completed by Artspace, a Twin Cities–based nonprofit corporation that has since become a leading developer of art-related projects nationwide. Working with the City of St. Paul and other public and private partners, Artspace converted the old warehouse into 52 studio-housing units for artists, some as large as 2,000 square feet.

24 Tilsner Artists' Cooperative (FOK Warehouse) N *L*

300 Broadway St.

Edward P. Bassford, 1894 / renovated, 1993

With its gorgeous orange brickwork and stately proportions, this Romanesque Revival–style building stands out from the

Lowertown crowd. Perhaps Bassford's best surviving work in St. Paul, it was built as a warehouse for the giant hardware wholesaling firm of Farwell, Ozmun and Kirk (FOK) and was later occupied by the Tilsner Box Co. The building was almost lost when a 1980s redevelopment plan went sour, leaving the struc-

Tilsner Artists' Cooperative

ture roofless and windowless for several years. Artspace and various partners then stepped in to undertake a renovation. The Tilsner has 66 "live-work units," as they're called, organized around two seven-story-high atriums that bring in natural light.

25 Chicago Great Western Freight Condominiums (Wisconsin Central Railway Freight Depot)

343–81 Kellogg Blvd. East

1901 / renovated, ca. 1980s

A railroad freight house converted into office condominiums.

POI B Trout Brook Canal

Fourth St. beneath and east of Lafayette Freeway (Hwy. 52) Bridge

George Wilson (engineer), 1891–94

Venture east past Broadway along Fifth St., then jog south to Fourth, and you'll encounter an urban remnant—a stone canal that carries Trout Brook beneath the railroad tracks east of Lowertown. The canal leads to a tunnel through which the brook then flows into Phalen Creek, also diverted underground here long ago. Trains still use the Trout Brook corridor to climb out of the Mississippi River Valley, but the number of tracks in use today is only a fraction of what it once was.

Great Northern Lofts

26 Great Northern (Railway Headquarters) Lofts ! N L

281–99 Kellogg Blvd. East

James Brodie, 1888 / two stories added, James Brodie, 1900 / renovated, Cermak Rhoades Architects, 2003

Architecturally and historically, one of Lowertown's most significant buildings. Now consisting of 53 luxurious condominiums, the building was once the headquarters of the Great Northern Railway and its chief executive, James J. Hill, who ran his railroad empire from a second-floor office. Like Hill, the building is rock solid and all business, and with its overscaled stone entrance on Kellogg and massive brick walls, it has the rather forbidding look of a Florentine palace. There's nothing else quite like it in Lowertown.

Part of what makes the building so distinctive is its structural system. Hill and his in-house architect, James Brodie, were obsessed by the Chicago fire of 1871 and took unusual steps to make the building fireproof. Instead of the typical iron or timber frame, the building has solid exterior and interior masonry walls (three feet thick in places), with steel beams supporting arched brick or clay ceilings. The building's massiveness was nearly its undoing. Pilings driven into the Lowertown muck failed at one corner, causing the structure to settle by as much as two feet.

A year before his death in 1916, Hill moved his headquarters to a new building a few blocks away at 180 East Fifth St. This building was then used for record storage and other purposes. It sat vacant for 30 years before its conversion into condominiums. The $30 million renovation included foundation repairs as well as restoration of some original features, among them an impressive wrought-iron staircase in the main lobby. The building's open courtyard, reached via an arched carriageway off Wall St., was also preserved.

27 Lowertown Lofts (Koehler and Hinrichs Co., Goff and Howard Building) N L

255 Kellogg Blvd. East

Louis Lockwood, 1901 / renovated, HGA, 1986

The first building in Lowertown to be converted into artists' cooperative housing. The 29 units are arranged around an atrium.

28 Main U.S. Post Office

180 Kellogg Blvd. East

Holabird and Root (Chicago) with Lambert Bassindale, 1934 / renovated and enlarged, Ellerbe Associates and Brooks Cavin, 1964

A rather grim art deco building finished in Mankato-Kasota stone and not nearly as elegant as its counterpart from the same period in Minneapolis. The postal service, which plans to open a new facility in suburban Eagan in 2010, put this building up for sale in late 2009.

POI C Lambert's (Lower) Landing (Lower Levee)

Jackson and Sibley Sts. at Mississippi River

1830s / rebuilt, Works Progress Administration, 1937 / renovated, ca. 1990s

In the early days of St. Paul, this was one of the nation's busiest steamboat landings. In 1858 alone, more than 1,000 boats docked here, delivering people and goods to the growing city. The steamboat trade quickly diminished after the Civil War with the arrival of railroads. Today, towboats and an occasional visiting cruise boat still use the landing.

Brooks Building

29 Brooks Building (Merchants National Bank) N *L*

366–68 Jackson St.

Edward P. Bassford, 1892 / renovated, ca. 1985

A richly ornamented Richardsonian Romanesque building, originally home to Merchants National Bank. It makes excellent use of the easily carved Lake Superior sandstone widely used by Twin Cities architects in the 1880s and 1890s. The small, partially restored lobby is worth a look, but the original banking hall is gone. The bank operated here until 1915, when it moved into a much larger new building at Fourth and Robert Sts.

30 180 East Fifth (Railroad and Bank Building) N *L*

176–80 East Fifth St.

Charles S. Frost (Chicago), 1916 / renovated, HGA, 1987

With a million square feet of floor space, this office building was the Twin Cities' largest until completion of the IDS Center in Minneapolis in 1973. It originally

180 East Fifth

housed the central offices of James J. Hill's Great Northern and Northern Pacific railroads as well as the First National Bank of St. Paul. The latter occupied a skylit banking hall at the bottom of the open light court in the building's center. Like Hill's office building on Kellogg Blvd., this one offers little in the way of architectural frills, although a few classical details can be found on the lower floors and at the cornice. Legend holds that the building was initially divided by a wall separating the two railroad offices, the only interior connection a door in Hill's office.

When the building was renovated for general office use in 1987, the old banking hall received a fashionable mauve and teal color scheme. What seemed like a good idea at the time in retrospect was a bit like dressing a burly laborer in drag. Hill would not have approved.

31 Straus Apartments (Noyes Brothers and Cutler Co. Building) N *L*

350–64 Sibley St.

1879 / additions (including fifth floor), 1900 / renovated, KKE Architects, 2003

The oldest commercial building in Lowertown, constructed for John Wann, a St. Paul businessman who hailed from Northern Ireland. Its first occupant was

Straus Apartments

Noyes Brothers and Cutler Co., a large wholesaling firm that later moved to the north side of Mears Park. The four-story building originally included a bracketed cornice, a shallow central pediment, and other ornamental details. These features have disappeared, but the building retains its prominent window hoods—a signature element of the Italianate style. Used for many years by the Straus Knitting Co., the building suffered a number of unsympathetic remodelings before being renovated for use as apartments in 2003.

32 Sibley Square (Gordon and Ferguson Co.) N L

333 Sibley St.

Clarence H. Johnston (C. A. P. Turner, engineer), 1913 / addition, Clarence H. Johnston, 1923

The youngest of Lowertown's historic warehouses, designed by prominent St. Paul architect Clarence Johnston for a company that specialized in fur and leather goods, now converted to offices. Like the Cosmopolitan across Mears Park, Sibley Square uses the concrete framing system patented by C. A. P. Turner. A thin appliqué of classical detailing does little to disguise the building's no-nonsense design.

33 Minnesota Telecenter L

172 East Fourth St.

HGA, 1988

A painfully dull building that serves as home to Twin Cities Public Television, which apparently didn't want to risk overstimulating its architectural audience. The coil-like steel sculptures on the roof remain one of the great design mysteries of Lowertown.

34 Union Depot Place (including Union Depot Lofts) ! N L

214 East Fourth St.

Charles S. Frost (Chicago), 1923 / renovated, Rafferty Rafferty Mikutowski Associates, 1983 / renovated, James Dayton Design, 2006

St. Paul's first Union Depot opened in 1881 directly below this one, at the foot of Sibley St., along the riverfront. Damaged by fire in 1884, it was rebuilt and survived until 1913, when it burned to the ground. After some haggling among the railroads, work on this mighty depot—a sober Beaux-Arts building with a monumental Doric colonnade—began in 1917.

The depot itself was only part of a $15 million project that included construction of a massive concrete rail platform to lift tracks 17 feet above the flood-prone Mississippi. (This platform in turn required construction of a new, higher Robert Street Bridge and rebuilding of the adjacent Chicago Great Western Railroad Lift Bridge.) To make room for the depot and its appurtenances, the railroads cleared away several

Union Depot Place

blocks of historic buildings, among them a hotel once operated by Marshall Sherman, who won the Medal of Honor at the Battle of Gettysburg.

The depot has two distinct sections. At the front is the main building, or head house, organized around a skylit lobby finished in polished marble and Mankato-Kasota stone. The skylights have been closed over; today's lobby is thus much darker than the original. To the rear, extending across Kellogg Blvd., is a long barrel-

Union Depot Place interior

vaulted concourse now closed to the public. The concourse offers one especially fetching detail in the form of a terra-cotta frieze depicting the history of transportation across the Upper Midwest. In the depot's glory years, as many as 20,000 passengers a day poured through the concourse, which led to 21 sets of tracks used by seven railroads. Trains—up to 140 daily—arrived and departed at all hours.

The last train pulled out in 1971. The old building was renovated by a hopeful developer in 1983 but never enjoyed much financial success. Beginning in 2005 the

upper floors of the head house were converted into 33 condominium units. Ambitious plans for returning local and regional rail service to the depot are afoot. Meanwhile, the magnificent concourse, now owned by Ramsey County, remains vacant.

35 American House Apartments (Western Supply Co. Warehouse) N *L*

352 Wacouta St.

Cass Gilbert, 1895 / renovated, Rafferty Rafferty Tollefson Lindeke Architects, 1986

Like the old shoe factory (now Parkside Apartments) next door, this building was commissioned by members of the Gotzian family. By the mid-1890s, Cass Gilbert was well into his classical period (as evidenced by his winning design for the new State Capitol), and here he produced a lovely little brick building that draws its inspiration from the Italian Renaissance. It served as a company outlet store but was later rented to other businesses. Now used for housing, the building was for many years known to St. Paulites as home of the American Beauty Macaroni Co.

36 262 Studios (Hackett Building) N *L*

262 East Fourth St.

Clarence H. Johnston, ca. 1900

This small, midblock building, now used for apartments, is all that remains of what was once one of Lowertown's finest warehouses, the Hackett Wholesale

Hardware Co. Designed by Clarence Johnston and opened in 1891, the Hackett Building extended all the way east to the corner of Wall St. Johnston designed this building as a stylistically identical addition to a larger structure, which was destroyed by fire in 1982.

37 Lot 270 Condominiums

270 East Fourth St.

Sherman Rutzick and Associates and Mendota Homes, Inc., 2005

One of the latest additions to Lowertown's stock of housing, designed in the usual nostalgic style.

38 Northwestern Building (Chicago, St. Paul, Minneapolis and Omaha Railroad Offices) N L

275 East Fourth St.

Charles S. Frost (Chicago), 1917

The now vanished "Omaha Railroad," as it was known in St. Paul, built this office structure for its own use. Architect Charles Frost was a favorite of railroad men, including James J. Hill, for whom he'd just completed a much larger office building at 180 East Fifth St. Frost also designed another Lowertown monument—Union Depot.

39 Parkside Apartments (Gotzian Shoe Co.) N L

242–50 East Fifth St.

Cass Gilbert, 1892 / 1905 / renovated, Bower Lewis Thrower Architects (Philadelphia), 1986

includes **J. H. Mahler Co. Building**, 258–60 East Fifth St.

1883

The Parkside was originally home to a shoe company founded by Conrad Gotzian, a German immigrant who was one of nineteenth-century St. Paul's success stories and also a close friend of James J. Hill. A shoemaker by trade, Gotzian arrived in St. Paul in the 1850s and at the time of his death in 1887 had built a shoe manufacturing and wholesale business employing more than 450 workers. Gotz-

ian's heirs planned this building, one of three surviving works in Lowertown by Cass Gilbert.

Although Gilbert is best known for his palatial State Capitol, he

Parkside Apartments

was an excellent designer of warehouses and other industrial buildings because of his sure sense of proportions and his skillful handling of large volumes. Here, he used windows grouped within broad recessed arches to create an especially pleasing structure reminiscent of the Chicago work of such architectural masters as H. H. Richardson and John Wellborn Root, Jr. Considered purely as a designed object, this may be Lowertown's best building.

Included in the renovated Parkside complex is the old J. H. Mahler Co. Building, originally home to a carriage dealer. The cast-iron columns on the ground floor were made by the Washington Foundry in St. Paul.

Mears Park Centre

40 Mears Park Centre N L

Fairbanks-Morse Co. Building, 220 East Fifth St.

J. Walter Stevens, 1895 / renovated, Winsor/Faricy Architects, 1988

Powers Dry Goods Co. Building, 230–36 East Fifth St.

J. Walter Stevens, 1892 / renovated, Winsor/Faricy Architects, 1988

Two sturdy warehouses, now used for offices. The Fairbanks-Morse Building is the more interesting of the two, offering a Renaissance Revival facade that is rather ornate by Lowertown's utilitarian standards.

41 Cosmopolitan Apartments (Finch, Van Slyck and McConville Co.) N L

366 Wacouta St.

James F. Denson (Chicago) with C. A. P. Turner, 1911 / 1915 / addition, Clarence H. Johnston, 1923 / renovated, Bower Lewis Thrower Architects (Philadelphia), 1986

Although this warehouse was built only a few years after Sommers Co. across Sixth St., it represents a giant leap forward in technology. The Sommers building relied on a time-honored system known as "mill construction," consisting of outer brick bearing walls tied to an interior frame of heavy timber. This warehouse, erected for a large

dry-goods wholesaler, was built of reinforced concrete using a slab-and-column system patented by Minneapolis engineer C. A. P. Turner. The concrete frame, first

Cosmopolitan Apartments

used in the Twin Cities around 1905, had many advantages for warehouse construction: tremendous strength, virtual invulnerability to fire, large free-span spaces, and room for many windows to bring in daylight for workers.

4 State Capitol Area

State Capitol Area

Until the 1890s, when work began on the present State Capitol, this part of St. Paul was a curious mix of splendor and squalor. A row of mansions crowning the hills along University and Sherburne avenues provided the splendor. Among them were the magnificent John Merriam House (1887), a brownstone fantasy that may have been the finest of all nineteenth-century mansions in St. Paul, and the towered George Benz House (1888). Other large homes and elegant apartment buildings clustered around Central Park, now the site of a parking ramp behind the Centennial Office Building.

Squalor, however, was nearby. Just to the east of the mansion district, in what is now the Mount Airy Housing Development, a tangle of short, steep streets and battered old houses formed a tough neighborhood sometimes called the "Badlands." To the south, where the Capitol Mall spreads out today, was a mixed commercial-residential zone that wasn't as impoverished as the Badlands but wasn't one of the city's garden spots either.

Virtually all traces of these historic neighborhoods are gone, largely as a result of two far-reaching decisions in city planning made half a century apart. The first came in 1893, when the state decided to build a new capitol on the so-called "Wabasha Street site"—a tract of land on what was then the northern fringes of downtown. This decision had two long-lasting consequences: it separated the center of state government from the center of St. Paul (the first two capitols had been located at Tenth and Wabasha streets not far from the downtown core) and it also doomed the hilltop mansions, which gave way one by one to the inevitable expansion of government offices. The process was slow, however, and the last of the great houses stood until the 1960s.

The second critical development in this area's history occurred in the 1940s. At that time, the capitol still lacked a formal setting, having only a small, oddly shaped patch of open lawn in front of it. Over the years there had been many proposals for a grand mall, including several (in 1903, 1909, and 1931) from the building's architect, Cass Gilbert. But it wasn't until 1944 that plans for a true mall finally began to move forward. In that year, a team consisting of Clarence H. Johnston, Jr., Edward Nelson, and Arthur Nichols prepared a design for the St. Paul City Planning Board that envisioned something very close to the current fan-shaped mall. The three planners also surmised, correctly, that a proposed federal highway (now Interstates 94–35E) would be routed south of the mall rather than to the north of the capitol building.

The 1944 plan, slightly modified a year later, was carried out in the early 1950s along with extensive redevelopment of adjoining areas east and west of the capitol. The new mall was a huge project that required sweeping away dozens of old buildings, including homes, apartments, churches, and shops. The project also completely reordered the historic streetscape around the capitol. Four new government structures—the Veterans Service Building, the Transportation Building, the Centennial Office Building, and a National Guard Armory—were then built around the mall in the 1950s and early 1960s.

A decade later, the transformation of the capitol area continued with construction of the interstate highway south of the mall. This rude trench filled with rushing traffic only reinforced the sense of separation between the capitol area and downtown. A route north of the capitol would have been much better, but downtown leaders didn't want the freeway to be built that far from the central business core. In the 1980s, efforts were made to undo some of the damage by redesigning a section of the freeway near the capitol to incorporate classically inspired bridges, walls, railings, lampposts, and other features. There was also a grand plan to rebuild the mall in a more formal neoclassical manner, but it fizzled for lack of money. The 1990s and early years of the twenty-first century saw another boom in state construction around the mall and just south of the interstate along Tenth and 11th streets. These recent buildings range in style from tepid exercises in faux classicism to more energetic modernist works. Overall, however, most of these newer works represent a missed opportunity to complement Gilbert's brilliant capitol building with modern architecture of real distinction.

Minnesota State Capitol

1 Minnesota State Capitol ! N

75 Rev. Dr. Martin Luther King Jr. Blvd.

Cass Gilbert, 1905 / restoration, Miller Dunwiddie Architects, 1983 and later / Art: Quadriga *(sculpture), Daniel Chester French and Edward C. Potter, 1906*

This gleaming marble palace has become such a familiar Minnesota icon that it's easy to take the building for granted, especially in view of its obvious similarities to other big public buildings (including numerous state capitols) of the time. Yet it really is an exceptional work in any number of respects, beginning with the fact that it's now famous architect, Cass Gilbert, was just 35 years old when he won a design competition for the building in 1895. That age is still very young in a profession where mastery tends to come late in life. Fortunately, Gilbert was wise beyond his years, and he produced for the people of Minnesota a remarkably rich and sophisticated work of architecture.

Gilbert was able to do so not just because he knew his pediments and pilasters but because he was so skilled at the fundamentals of architecture. The capitol showcases all of Gilbert's strengths—his sure command of form and proportion, his careful handling of materials, his talent as an ornamentalist, his ability

Minnesota State Capitol interior

to orchestrate a "total design" with a team of artists and craftsmen, even his sense of humor, evident in such whimsical details as the gophers and loons that inhabit the capitol's decorative bronzework.

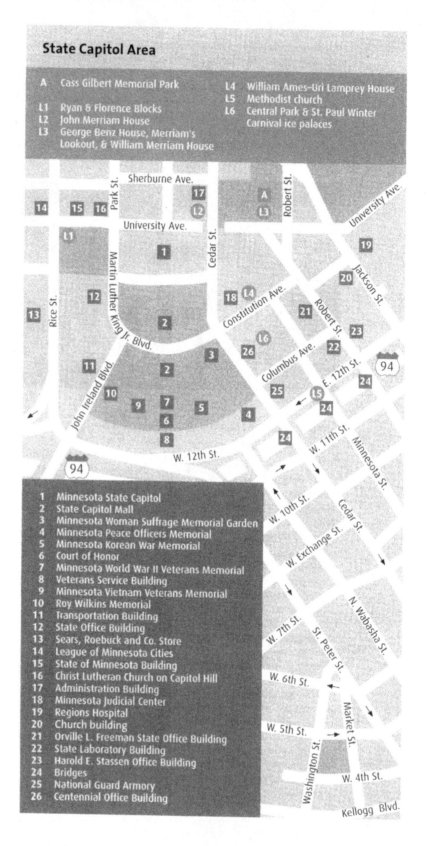

State Capitol Area

A   Cass Gilbert Memorial Park

L1   Ryan & Florence Blocks
L2   John Merriam House
L3   George Benz House, Merriam's
     Lookout, & William Merriam House

L4   William Ames–Uri Lamprey House
L5   Methodist church
L6   Central Park & St. Paul Winter
     Carnival ice palaces

1   Minnesota State Capitol
2   State Capitol Mall
3   Minnesota Woman Suffrage Memorial Garden
4   Minnesota Peace Officers Memorial
5   Minnesota Korean War Memorial
6   Court of Honor
7   Minnesota World War II Veterans Memorial
8   Veterans Service Building
9   Minnesota Vietnam Veterans Memorial
10   Roy Wilkins Memorial
11   Transportation Building
12   State Office Building
13   Sears, Roebuck and Co. Store
14   League of Minnesota Cities
15   State of Minnesota Building
16   Christ Lutheran Church on Capitol Hill
17   Administration Building
18   Minnesota Judicial Center
19   Regions Hospital
20   Church building
21   Orville L. Freeman State Office Building
22   State Laboratory Building
23   Harold E. Stassen Office Building
24   Bridges
25   National Guard Armory
26   Centennial Office Building

The mere fact that Gilbert was able to get the building he wanted testifies to his force of will—an essential character trait for any ambitious architect. Large works of public architecture almost always generate controversy, and the capitol was no exception. One of the biggest brouhahas centered on Gilbert's desire to dress the capitol in snowy white marble from Georgia. Minnesota's quarrymen thought such a lucrative contract should stay within the state. In the end, Gilbert got his marble after agreeing to build the capitol's base of St. Cloud granite and to use other Minnesota stone inside the building.

The capitol has one other quality seldom remarked on. Although it's large and sumptuous in the usual Beaux-Arts manner, it's not as relentlessly overwhelming as some other state capitols of the period—Wisconsin's, say, or Pennsylvania's. In other words, Gilbert's building seems to be just the right size—big enough to show off the majesty of the state but not so large as to seem, well, swollen-headed in a very un-Minnesotan way. Gilbert struck close to a perfect balance here—no small accomplishment.

Like other major public buildings of its era, the capitol is chock-full of art in the form of paintings, sculpture, and all manner of hortatory inscriptions designed to encourage noble thinking. Much of this high-minded art seems quaint today, but it adds considerably to the building's charm. The one

piece of art that has something like an architectural function is the famous *Quadriga*, officially entitled *The Progress of the State*, sculpted by Daniel Chester French and Edward C. Potter. Positioned at the base of the dome, these muscular horses add a note of vital, golden energy to Gilbert's otherwise classically serene building.

Over the years, the capitol suffered from its share of inept remodelings and benign neglect, but in the 1980s, under the leadership of Gov. Rudy Perpich, the state finally began to treat the building with the respect it deserves. Most major spaces have been restored, and a carefully developed preservation plan now guides all renovation work. Gilbert undoubtedly would be pleased.

Because the capitol is so large and so packed with architectural detail, it's best seen by taking one of the regularly scheduled tours or by wandering around yourself with the aid of a book such as Thomas O'Sullivan's excellent *North Star Statehouse: An Armchair Guide to the Minnesota State Capitol.*

2 State Capitol Mall

Area bounded by Rev. Dr. Martin Luther King Jr. Blvd., Cedar St., 12th St., and John Ireland Blvd.

Clarence H. Johnston, Jr., Edward Nelson, Morrell and Nichols (George Nason), 1950–54 and later

Something like the mall as it exists today was envisioned as far

State Capitol Mall

back as 1902, when Cass Gilbert drew the first of his many plans for such a project. His modest sketch blossomed over time into more grandiose schemes. His last plan, in 1931, proposed a vast mall that would have marched down from the capitol like one of Baron Haussmann's famous Parisian boulevards, circled around a war memorial column near today's Interstate 94–35E corridor, sliced through Seven Corners and Irvine Park, and crossed the Mississippi River on a new bridge before terminating in a traffic circle atop the West Side bluffs at Smith Ave. A wonderful dream, but it had no hope of becoming reality in those dark financial days, if ever.

The mall that finally was built after World War II has always been a disappointment. For all of its size, it's not especially grand, and except for a few special occasions it receives little public use. Size, in fact, is part of its problem: big and diffuse, it bleeds past the edges of the state buildings that make a futile effort to define and contain it.

Over the years, various proposals to remake the mall have come and gone. Chicago architect Helmut Jahn produced a brilliant scheme in the 1970s to build parking and new office space beneath the mall, where a system of tunnels connecting the capitol and other buildings was already in place. In the 1980s the state conducted a competition to redesign the mall. The winning entry called for a classically inspired series of plazas, gardens, and walls that would have given the mall a much more formal appearance. But this decidedly Gilbertian dream, like Jahn's proposal, failed for lack of financing.

In the 1990s, the mall began to take on a new dimension as home to memorials honoring significant people and events. Five were built between 1992 and 2000 and more are in the works. While they're generally well designed, these commemorative spaces have given the mall an increasingly funereal feel at a time

when what it really needs is more liveliness and less embalmed solemnity.

In keeping with its status as Minnesota's formal front yard, the mall also offers a variety of public art, mostly of the heroic sculptural variety. Major works include *John Albert Johnson Memorial* (statue), Andrew J. O'Connor, Jr., 1912 (Johnson was governor of Minnesota from 1904 until he died of cancer in 1909); *Knute Nelson Memorial* (statue), John Karl Daniels, 1928 (Nelson represented Minnesota in the U.S. Senate from 1895 until his death in 1923); *Memorial to Christopher Columbus* (statue), Charles Brioschi, 1931; *Monument to the Living* (sculpture), Roger M. Brodin, 1982; *Charles A. Lindbergh Memorial* (statue), Paul Granlund, 1985; *Memorial to Floyd B. Olson* (statue), Amerigo Brioschi, 1958 (Olson was a popular governor who died while in office in 1936); and *Memorial to Leif Erickson* (statue), John Karl Daniels, 1949.

3 Minnesota Woman Suffrage Memorial Garden ("The Garden of Time")

Rev. Dr. Martin Luther King Jr. Blvd. and Cedar St.

Art: Loom, *Ralph Nelson and Raveevarn Choksombatchi, 2000*

A pleasant green place at the northeast corner of the mall that includes a timeline of the suffrage movement incorporated into a metal trellis.

4 Minnesota Peace Officers Memorial

Near 12th and Wabasha Sts.

Ankeny Kell Architects (Fred Richter), 1995

A classically inspired memorial honoring law enforcement officers who died in the line of duty.

5 Minnesota Korean War Memorial

East of Court of Honor near center of mall

Bob Kost and Dean Olson with Art Norby, 1998

Statuary and stone markers list the names of 700 Minnesotans who died in the Korean War.

6 Court of Honor

North of Veterans Service Building

Johnston, Nelson, and Nichols, 1951

A semicircular plaza with plaques describing Minnesotans' service in the nation's wars.

7 Minnesota World War II Veterans Memorial

Between Veterans Service Building and capitol

Craig Amundsen and Ben Sporer, Bryan D. Carlson and Myklebust-Sears, 2007

An oval-shaped granite plaza with etched-glass panels narrating Minnesotans' role in World War II.

Veterans Service Building

8 Veterans Service Building

20 West 12th St.

Brooks Cavin, 1954 / 1973 / Art: Promise of Youth (statue), Alonzo Hauser, 1958

The best post–World War II building on the mall and one of the city's first truly modern works of architecture. It has been criti-cized for standing square in the middle of Cass Gilbert's grand vista; however, by the time the building was planned, Gilbert's dream of a mighty boulevard marching south from the mall was long since dead. A fairer criticism might be that the Veterans Building, with its bridgelike structure and rather quiet presence, isn't monumental enough to effectively terminate the north-south axis that connects it visually to the capitol.

That said, the building is a fine work from a time when most American architects were enthralled with the clean lines and crisp detailing of the International Style. The granite-clad building features two low wings connected by a three-story "bridge" that spans an open plaza, a gesture toward preserving Gilbert's beloved vista. Among the building's most pleasant amenities is a top-floor cafeteria that offers views of the capitol.

9 Minnesota Vietnam Veterans Memorial (*Lakefront DMZ*)

West of Court of Honor

Nina Ackerberg, Jake Castillo, Rich Laffin, and Stanton Sears, 1992

A sunken plaza featuring a map of Minnesota and a granite wall incised with the names of soldiers killed or missing in Vietnam. The design was clearly influenced by Maya Lin's celebrated Vietnam Memorial in Washington, DC.

Minnesota Vietnam Veterans Memorial

10 Roy Wilkins Memorial (*Spiral for Justice*)

Along John Ireland Blvd.

Curtis Patterson, 1995

The mall's most peculiar memorial, using copper-clad walls, pyramids, and other exotic elements to celebrate the achievements of Roy Wilkins, a civil rights leader raised in St. Paul. The effect, however, is vaguely unsettling: knowing nothing of the memorial's true purpose, visitors might think they have wandered into the open-air temple of a religious cult.

Transportation Building

11 Transportation (State Highway Department) Building

395 John Ireland Blvd.

Ellerbe Architects, 1957 / renovated, Wold Architects, 1994–2000

A better work than the contemporaneous Centennial Office Building across the mall but still very much in the all-purpose corporate style of the 1950s. The main lobby holds one welcome surprise: a "floating" staircase that's among the most elegant architectural details of its period in the Twin Cities.

12 State Office Building

100 Rev. Dr. Martin Luther King Jr. Blvd.

Clarence H. Johnston, 1932 / remodeled and top floor added, Leo Lundgren Architects, 1986 / parking ramp, BWBR Architects, 1988

Not a great building, but, like Johnston's earlier Historical Society (now Judicial Center) on the other side of the mall, its restrained classicism nicely complements the State Capitol. Inside, you'll find a characteristic 1930s mix of art deco and classical elements. The building was revamped and a seventh floor added in the 1980s, when the parking ramp to the rear was also built.

13 Sears, Roebuck and Co. Store

425 Rice St.

1962

A suburban-style department store from the 1960s plunked down within eyeshot of the State Capitol. How, you wonder, did it happen? The answer is that the area west of Rice St. here was part of the city's first federally funded urban renewal project, approved in 1953. The site was cleared and then sold to Sears in 1956, prompting two unsuccessful lawsuits by downtown retail interests worried that the new store would hurt their sales. The store itself won't make you tingle with admiration, but it's far superior to the cheap stucco boxes typically built by retailers today.

LOST 1 *Where University Ave. and Rice St. cross was for many years a five-cornered intersection, with Wabasha St. entering at an angle from the southeast. A pair of colorful buildings, the **Ryan Block,** built in about 1890, and the mansard-roofed **Florence Block,** constructed in 1880, stood along Wabasha. In 1932, however, both buildings were demolished to make way for the State Office Building, and the intersection lost much of its character. Later, portions of Wabasha were also vacated, and the street now ends at the southern boundary of the Capitol Mall.*

14 League of Minnesota Cities

145 University Ave. West

Buetow and Associates, 1995

A clumsy attempt at an architectural statement, complete with a tower, oversized arches, and an underwhelming ground floor that looks to have been the victim of serious budget cuts.

15 State of Minnesota (Ford) Building

117 University Ave. West

John Graham (Seattle) with Kees and Colburn, 1914

This building began its life as a subassembly plant and service center for Ford Motel T automobiles. It even included a special tile roof on which vehicles could be tested, secure behind a nine-foot-high parapet. At its peak the plant turned out only about 500 cars annually, far fewer than did a much larger plant Ford built in Minneapolis the same year. Assembly ended at both buildings by 1924, when Ford completed a new plant in the Highland Park neighborhood of St. Paul. The building is now owned by the State of Minnesota.

16 Christ Lutheran Church on Capitol Hill (Norwegian Evangelical Lutheran Church)

105 University Ave. West

Buechner and Orth, 1913

Standing in the shadow of the State Capitol, this twin-towered building is a nice example of a small Renaissance Revival–style church. Built of yellow brick and white stone trim, the church's temple front features a pair of colossal Ionic columns rising from pedestals. The towers to either side culminate in open belfries in the form of miniature temples complete with Tuscan columns, pediments, and copper-clad caps surmounted by ball finials. The church is still home to the congregation that built it, although it was originally known as the Norwegian Evangelical Lutheran Church. That name was changed to Christ Lutheran Church in about 1918.

17 Administration Building

50 Sherburne Ave.

Ellerbe Associates, 1966

A marble-clad bureaucratic box from the 1960s, notable less for its own pompous presence than for what it replaced.

John Merriam House, 1895

LOST 2 *This was the site of the* **John Merriam House,** *designed by the architectural team of Charles W. Mould and Robert McNicol with a possible assist from Harvey Ellis. At once powerful and playful, the mansion, completed in 1887, was a nationally significant example of the Richardsonian Romanesque style. The St. Paul Institute (ancestor of today's Science Museum of Minnesota) bought the house in 1927. After the museum moved away in 1964, the state acquired the house and demolished it.*

POI A Cass Gilbert Memorial Park

Sherburne Ave. east of Cedar St.

ca. 1970s

An outthrust concrete overlook is the main feature of this park, which occupies some of the most intriguing ground in St. Paul.

LOST 3 *A row of mansions, including the* **George Benz House,** *once lined the hilltop here along Sherburne Ave., which ended in a cul-de-sac known as* **Merriam's Lookout.** *Set above a curving stone wall reached by a staircase, the lookout was a favorite vantage point. The wall and staircase were buried under fill when the area was cleared in the 1950s. The top of the wall can still be seen near the edge of the hill, and parts of the staircase are visible along Robert St. below. Nearby is a stone wall along Cedar St. that was once part of the estate of William Merriam (John's son, and governor of Minnesota from 1889 to 1893). The* **William Merriam House,** *built in 1882, stood*

Merriam's Lookout, 1895

east of Cedar and was among the neighborhood's earliest mansions.

18 Minnesota Judicial Center (Minnesota Historical Society)

25 Rev. Dr. Martin Luther King Jr. Blvd. (at Cedar St.)

*Clarence H. Johnston, 1918 / addition and renovation, Leonard Parker Associates, 1989 / includes **East Capitol Plaza**, Richard Fleischner, 1990 / Art: **Falling Water** (skylight), Pat Benning and Michael Pilla, 1995*

The original part of this building, at first home to the state historical society, is a solid if less than scintillating exercise in the heavy-duty classicism common to American public buildings of the era. Though it served well enough as a sober gray foil to the State Capitol, the building was significantly improved in 1989 with the addition of wings to the north and east housing judicial chambers and other court-related offices. At the same time, the original building was remodeled to accommodate new court- and hearing rooms.

The richly detailed addition is one of the high points of postmodern design in Minnesota. Especially notable is the north wing, the working quarters of the state's supreme court jus-

tices and other appellate judges. Arranged around a semicircle, the offices overlook a formal plaza designed by artist Richard Fleischner and the capitol itself (where the supreme court still hears cases). This visual relationship is beautifully worked out, as is the addition as a whole.

LOST 4 *Lost buildings on this site include the **William Ames–Uri Lamprey House,** a Greek Revival-style building from the 1850s that was expanded into one of the city's great Victorian extravaganzas in the 1880s.*

19 Regions Hospital

640 Jackson St.

Ellerbe Associates, 1965 / addition, 1977 / enlarged and renovated, BWBR Architects, 2001 / addition, Ellerbe Becket, 2009

This medical complex, long known as St. Paul–Ramsey, evolved out of a public hospital founded in 1872. Regions has sprawled every which way over the years but has not managed to achieve any memorable architecture in the process.

20 Church building (Central Park United Methodist)

639 Jackson St.

Haarstick and Lundgren, 1960

Minnesota Judicial Center

This was until 2009 home to St. Paul's oldest Protestant congregation, founded in 1848 as Market Street Methodist Church. The most distinctive feature of this

Central Park United Methodist Church

rather odd stone-and-brick structure is a rounded meeting room in front that calls to mind a Pullman car. The congregation, which joined with Wesley United Methodist in Minneapolis in 2007, has relocated to the city's West Side.

LOST 5 *Before moving into this building, the Central Methodist congregation worshiped in a fine stone* **church** *at 12th and Minnesota Sts. That church, dating to 1887, was demolished in 1961 to make way for Interstate 94.*

21 Orville L. Freeman State Office Building

625 North Robert St.

HGA and Pickard Chilton, 2005

With its bold play of vertical and horizontal elements and the spatial complexity of its facade, this building has a certain swagger to it. And it's about time. Although purists may shudder, it's downright refreshing to see a major building in the capitol complex that isn't content to be just another deferential box.

22 State Laboratory Building (Minnesota Departments of Agriculture and Health)

601 North Robert St.

HGA with CUH2A (Princeton, NJ), 2005

This building looks a bit like an oversized suburban branch bank from the 1960s, but at least it doesn't pursue the ghost of classicism.

23 Harold E. Stassen Office Building (Minnesota Department of Revenue)

600 North Robert St.

HGA and Ryan Construction, 1998

A sort of "classical light" building— competent but uninteresting.

24 Bridges

Cedar, Minnesota, Robert, and other downtown streets across Interstate 94–35E

David Mayernik and Thomas N. Rajkovich with HGA, 1987–92

The classically inspired bridges, walls, and railings along the interstate corridor were built to complement the State Capitol and its surroundings, and they're certainly an improvement over their predecessors. Still, it's hard to get too enthusiastic about this classicized stretch of freeway. The cast-stone detailing tends to be crude, and, while the state deserves credit for its good intentions, the bridges and other structures—gatehouses, obelisks, and the like—simply aren't convincing as classical designs.

Orville L. Freeman State Office Building (right) and State Laboratory Building

St. Paul Winter Carnival ice palace, 1886

25 National Guard Armory

600 Cedar St.

P. C. Bettenburg, 1961

There has been talk of demolishing this bland product of the 1960s. The idea should be encouraged.

26 Centennial Office Building

658 Cedar St.

Thorshov and Cerny, 1958

This long gray architectural filing cabinet is unworthy of its prime site on the mall, but it does offer a better quality of materials, from its heavy granite facing to its aluminum window spandrels, than you'll find on the newer state buildings nearby. As its name indicates, the building opened in 1958 as Minnesota was celebrating the 100th anniversary of statehood; its businesslike demeanor is just what you'd expect from a public building of that era.

*LOST 6 A parking ramp constructed behind the Centennial Building in 1974 occupies the site of **Central Park,** once a beautiful little urban square. The park, dating from 1884, included a small central fountain and was home to the first three **St. Paul Winter Carnival ice palaces,** built in 1886, 1887, and 1888. The historic homes and apartments around it were demolished in the 1950s and 1960s, and the park was little more than a vacant lot by the time the ramp was built.*

The Near West Side, West Seventh Street, and Irvine Park

Although these five areas aren't officially part of downtown St. Paul, they are all within a 15-minute walk from the central core and well worth a visit. Raspberry Island is home to a pair of notable structures—one a century old and the other quite new. On the West Side Flats you'll find a nineteenth-century stone bridge, caves, and one of the city's oldest riverfront parks, among other attractions. The portion of West Seventh Street next to downtown is a popular shopping and restaurant district that offers fine examples of Victorian commercial architecture. Just off Seventh is Irvine Park, a charming residential enclave with many of the city's oldest houses. The Upper Landing includes a park and a large housing development on the site of a historic riverfront community known as "Little Italy."

Raspberry (Navy) Island

This 2.2-acre island beneath the Wabasha Street Bridge was once one of several along this part of the Mississippi River. Fairly wild and wooded at one time, the island took its present shape in 1948 when the U.S. Navy built a reserve training facility on the eastern side. The navy left in 1968. The western portion of the island has been owned since 1872 by the Minnesota Boat Club. Today, Raspberry Island, which can be reached from the Wabasha Street Bridge and from Harriet Island Park, is home to a new park, the historic Minnesota Boat Club boathouse, and a band shell built for the Schubert Club of St. Paul.

Minnesota Boat Club

POI A Raspberry Island Park

City of St. Paul Division of Parks and Recreation, 2008

Long a rather scruffy, barren place, the island received a $5 million makeover in 2007–8. A limestone plaza, walkways, an aspen grove, an event lawn, and public restrooms were among the many improvements.

1 Minnesota Boat Club N *L*

Raspberry Island (1 South Wabasha St.)

George H. Carsley, 1910

Founded in 1870, the Minnesota Boat Club is the state's oldest athletic organization. This building is the club's second on the island, replacing a wooden structure erected in 1885. The boathouse, a fairly simple version in the Spanish Mission Revival style

Schubert Club Heilmaier Memorial Bandstand

popular in the early 1900s, contains storage on the ground level for the club's rowing shells and other equipment. The upper floor was originally used as a meeting and dining room; in later years it was leased out. Occupants included a memorably rough-and-tumble drinking establishment known as the River Serpent. A survivor of many floods, the boathouse continues to serve as the club's headquarters.

2 Schubert Club Heilmaier Memorial Bandstand

Raspberry Island

James Carpenter Design Associates, 2002

The most poetic object on St. Paul's riverfront, a sensuous sweep of laminated glass and stainless steel that, in Carpenter's words, "float[s] like a volume of light on the Mississippi River." The less poetically inclined might liken it to the billowing canvas top of a Conestoga wagon. Technically, the saddle-shaped roof is a hyperbolic paraboloid, but you don't have to be a mathematician to appreciate its elegance and grace. The $2 million structure was built largely with private funds raised by the Schubert Club of St. Paul.

West Side Flats

The Wabasha and Robert Street bridges cross over to the so-called West Side Flats, which in their natural state were pure floodplain, subject to annual inundations. For this reason, the flats attracted mostly poor immigrants—Germans and Irish, followed by East European Jews and Mexicans. There was once a complete urban world here that included homes, apartments, churches and synagogues, schools, stores, restaurants, and saloons. There were also large industries such as the Towle Co. (makers of the original Log Cabin syrup) and American Hoist and Derrick Co. (later Amhoist Corp.). Early on, sandstone bluffs proved useful to brewers, who carved out large cave systems to cool their beer. Other man-made caves were used to grow mushrooms and to age cheese.

Little of the historic flats community remains today. Following a disastrous flood in 1952, the city built new levees and then began clearing much of the area to create Riverview Industrial Park. Scores of properties were knocked down to make way for new industrial and commercial buildings set within a suburbanized landscape of lawns and parking lots. With few exceptions, the flats' modern-era architecture is of little interest. A few historic structures remain, however, including the Clarence W. Wigington Pavilion (1941), the Colorado Street Bridge (1888), and the tower of St. Michael's Church (1882), better known by its Spanish name, Torre de San Miguel.

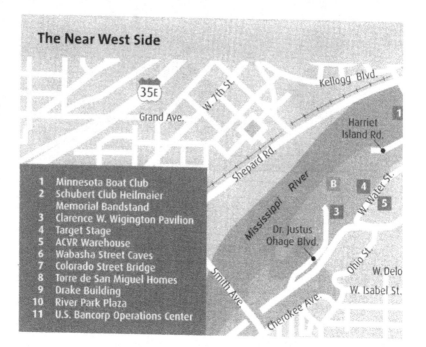

The Near West Side

1   Minnesota Boat Club
2   Schubert Club Heilmaier
    Memorial Bandstand
3   Clarence W. Wigington Pavilion
4   Target Stage
5   ACVR Warehouse
6   Wabasha Street Caves
7   Colorado Street Bridge
8   Torre de San Miguel Homes
9   Drake Building
10 River Park Plaza
11 U.S. Bancorp Operations Center

POI B Harriet Island Park

South Wabasha and Water Sts.

1900 / rebuilt, Wallace Roberts and Todd (Philadelphia) and St. Paul Division of Parks and Recreation, 2000

Despite its name, this riverfront park isn't an island. However, it was just that when purchased in 1900 by Dr. Justus Ohage, then St. Paul's public health officer. A great believer in parks as well as a civic philanthropist, Ohage outfitted the island with a bathhouse, playground, zoo, and other attractions before donating it to the city. The baths were a success, drawing as many as 25,000 people on hot summer days, but had to be closed for good in 1919 when the Mississippi became too polluted for swimming. The park, prone to flooding, proved difficult to maintain, and in 1949 the narrow channel on the island's south side was filled in. Another change came in 1964 when the West Side levee was completed to provide flood protection for the new Riverview Industrial Park. The levee was raised an additional four feet in 1994.

After languishing for many years, the park was rebuilt in the late 1990s as part of St. Paul's riverfront renewal effort. Improvements included a riverwalk, an enlarged public dock, and a new pedestrian gateway along with two significant architectural projects: renovation of the park's

West Side Flats, 1885

The Near West Side

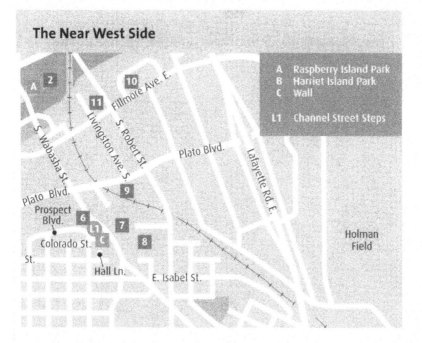

A	Raspberry Island Park
B	Harriet Island Park
C	Wall
L1	Channel Street Steps

1941 pavilion and construction of a new bandstand. River craft that dock at the park include the University of Minnesota Centennial Showboat and a 1940s-vintage towboat that has been renovated into a bed and breakfast called the Covington Inn.

3 Clarence W. Wigington Pavilion

200 Dr. Justus Ohage Blvd.

St. Paul City Architect (Charles A. Bassford with Clarence Wigington), 1941 / restored, Rafferty Rafferty Tollefson, 2000

Built under the auspices of the federal Works Progress Adminis-tration, this sturdy pavilion is Moderne in style but has a vaguely traditional feel. Its designer and namesake, Clarence Wigington, was the first black man in the United States to serve as a municipal architect. He worked as a draftsman and later as chief designer for the St. Paul City Architect's Office from 1915 until his retirement in 1949. The pavilion is also of interest because the Mankato-Kasota stone used in its construction was salvaged from the old St. Paul City Hall–Ramsey County Courthouse, built in 1889 and demolished in 1933.

Clarence W. Wigington Pavilion

Near West Side

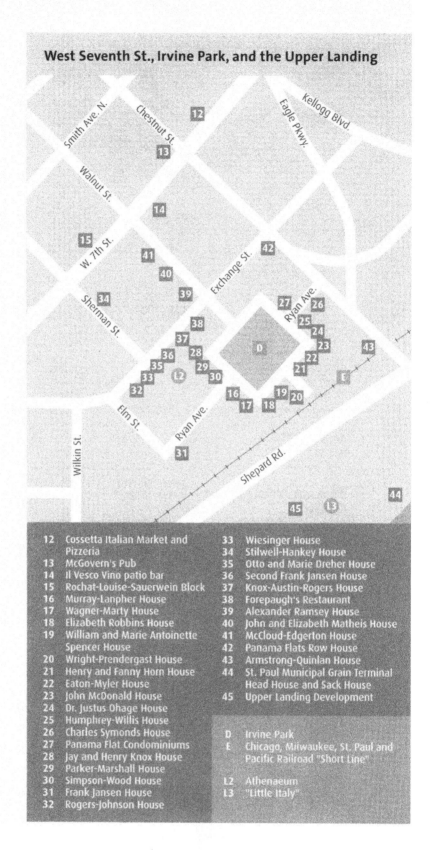

West Seventh St., Irvine Park, and the Upper Landing

12	Cossetta Italian Market and Pizzeria
13	McGovern's Pub
14	Il Vesco Vino patio bar
15	Rochat-Louise-Sauerwein Block
16	Murray-Lanpher House
17	Wagner-Marty House
18	Elizabeth Robbins House
19	William and Marie Antoinette Spencer House
20	Wright-Prendergast House
21	Henry and Fanny Horn House
22	Eaton-Myler House
23	John McDonald House
24	Dr. Justus Ohage House
25	Humphrey-Willis House
26	Charles Symonds House
27	Panama Flat Condominiums
28	Jay and Henry Knox House
29	Parker-Marshall House
30	Simpson-Wood House
31	Frank Jansen House
32	Rogers-Johnson House
33	Wiesinger House
34	Stilwell-Hankey House
35	Otto and Marie Dreher House
36	Second Frank Jansen House
37	Knox-Austin-Rogers House
38	Forepaugh's Restaurant
39	Alexander Ramsey House
40	John and Elizabeth Matheis House
41	McCloud-Edgerton House
42	Panama Flats Row House
43	Armstrong-Quinlan House
44	St. Paul Municipal Grain Terminal Head House and Sack House
45	Upper Landing Development

D	Irvine Park
E	Chicago, Milwaukee, St. Paul and Pacific Railroad "Short Line"
L2	Athenaeum
L3	"Little Italy"

4 Target Stage

Harriet Island Park

Michael Graves and Associates, 2001

Graves built his reputation as a postmodern theorist and architect but has become better known of late as a designer of household items for Target Corp. This bandstand, which looks like a pair of oil derricks in search of some crude, is not one of his finer moments. The idea apparently was to evoke the industrial history of the flats as well as the truss work of the old Smith Avenue High Bridge. The whole thing comes across as pompous overkill, while the stage itself has proved to be of dubious utility.

5 ACVR Warehouse (FOK Building)

102–6 West Water St.

1911 / addition, 1915

One of the oldest buildings left on the flats. Its original owner was Farwell, Ozmun and Kirk Co., a hardware wholesaler. Many artists now occupy the building.

Wabasha Street Caves, 1933

6 Wabasha Street Caves (Castle Royal Nightclub)

215 South Wabasha St.

ca. 1890s / converted to nightclub, Myrtus Wright, 1933 / renovated, 1975 and later

St. Paul's most celebrated underground establishment, once home to the Castle Royal nightclub. The caves—a series of interconnected tunnels excavated out of St. Peter sandstone in the nineteenth century—were mined for silica and later used to grow mushrooms. In 1933 William Lehman, son-in-law to the caves' first owner, turned them into a nightclub.

Lehman hired architect Myrtus Wright to design a castlelike brick facade over the entrances. Inside, the club had two bars and fixtures scavenged from the demolished Charles Gates mansion in Minneapolis.

Modestly billed as the "World's Most Gorgeous Underground Nite Club," the Castle Royal quickly became one of the city's hot spots. Stories, some of them no doubt embroidered, tell of gangsters, gun molls, and other disreputable characters frolicking to the music of bandleaders like Cab Calloway and Harry James. By 1940, however, the club was losing money and closed. Today, the caves are rented out for a variety of special events and tours are available.

Channel Street Steps, 2007

LOST 1 *The **Channel Street (Hall Avenue) Steps**, St. Paul's tallest public staircase, consisting of a freestanding tower attached to the blufftop by a small bridge, stood next to the Wabasha Street Caves from 1916 to 2008, when it was damaged by falling rocks and had to be taken down. A replacement— also painted green—should be under construction by 2010.*

POI C Wall

South Wabasha St. near Wabasha Street Caves

City of St. Paul Department of Public Works and Seitu Jones (artist), 2005

An undulating concrete retaining wall that doubles as an art object.

Near West Side

Colorado Street Bridge, Torre de San Miguel at right

It features a decorative steel railing and the word for *home* inscribed in 12 languages.

7 Colorado Street Bridge N

East side of South Wabasha St. about three blocks south of Plato Blvd.

Andreas Munster, 1888

A historic masonry bridge built to carry Colorado St. across Starkey St. but now used only by pedestrians. The bridge required a tricky angled crossing, so assistant city engineer Andreas Munster designed alternating stone and brick courses that run the length of the arch rather than in the traditional crosswise manner. Munster's design was daring: as a precaution, he left wooden centering beneath the arch for a year after the bridge opened.

8 Torre de San Miguel Homes

58 Wood St. (between Wabasha and Robert Sts. south of Plato Blvd.)

St. Paul Housing Authority, 1968 / enlarged, Fishman and Associates, ca. 1980 / renovated, ca. 1990s / includes St. Michael's Catholic Church tower, 1882

An unremarkable modern housing project except for the church tower after which it's named. The bell tower, Italian in character, is all that remains of the old St. Michael's Catholic Church, demolished in 1970. The tower is the flats' oldest surviving work of architecture.

9 Drake Building (Drake Marble Co.)

60 Plato Blvd. East

1909 / renovated, MS&R Architects, 2002

A sleek makeover of an early twentieth-century concrete-frame industrial building into offices. The architects refaced the exterior with corrugated metal in sassy colors, added a stair and elevator tower, and topped it all with a bold sign. The result is a crisp, clean design that calls to mind the work of the German Bauhaus.

10 River Park Plaza

10 River Park Plaza (off Fillmore St. near Robert St.)

Pope Associates, 1988

At ten stories, this angular, glass-clad office structure is the tallest building on the West Side Flats. It's not badly done, but it feels out of place along the riverfront.

11 U.S. Bancorp Operations Center

60 Livingston Ave.

Opus Architects, 2003

A brick office complex that in its apparent desire to not offend anyone manages to avoid even the tiniest spark of architectural inspiration.

West Seventh Street from Seven Corners to Grand Ave.

West Seventh, also known as Fort Rd., is one of the city's oldest streets. Its present course was established in the 1850s (before then, an early version ran along the blufftops above the river), providing an essential link between downtown St. Paul and Fort Snelling. By 1891, streetcar lines extended the full length of West Seventh. Today, the street is almost entirely commercial in the Seven Corners area, where it's become the centerpiece of what might be called St. Paul's "old town"—an eclectic collection of bars, restaurants, antique shops, and other businesses, many occupying historic buildings. It's an irony worth noting that this little commercial district, once considered to be a marginal area crowded with dumpy old buildings, is now the liveliest place downtown, especially on nights when the Minnesota Wild play at the Xcel arena. One secret of its success is that it largely avoided the soul-crushing urban renewal of the 1960s and later that rendered so much of downtown sterile.

12 Cossetta Italian Market and Pizzeria

211 West Seventh St.

1883 and later

The taller of the two buildings that make up this popular eatery dates to 1883 and is one of the oldest along this part of Seventh. Its builder, James Gilfillan, also happened to be chief justice of the Minnesota Supreme Court, a position that in those days does not seem to have been quite as exalted as it is now.

McGovern's Pub

13 McGovern's Pub (Smith Block)

225 West Seventh St.

Edward P. Bassford, 1888

Robert A. Smith, mayor of St. Paul from 1887 to 1902 and for whom nearby Smith Ave. is named, erected this Romanesque Revival–style brick building. The cast panels above the second-floor windows depict the mythical horse Pegasus, while those above the third show a woman's face against a back-

ground of scrolls and garlands. The building's designer, Edward P. Bassford, was among St. Paul's most prominent nineteenth-century architects.

Il Vesco Vino patio bar

14 Il Vesco Vino patio bar (Justus Ramsey House) N L

242 West Seventh St.

ca. 1857

This tiny Greek Revival cottage, with stone walls two feet thick, was built as a rental property by Justus Ramsey. He was the brother and business partner of Alexander Ramsey, Minnesota's first territorial governor, whose considerably more spacious stone home is a block away. Justus Ramsey lost ownership of the cottage after the financial crash of 1857, and the property went through many owners before being purchased by an antiques dealer in the 1930s. It is now what must surely be the most historic patio bar in Minnesota.

Rochat-Louise-Sauerwein Block

15 Rochat-Louise-Sauerwein Block N L

261–77 West Seventh St.

Rochat Building, William H. Castner, 1885 / Louise Building, Edward P. Bassford, 1885 / Sauerwein Building, Hermann Kretz, 1895

It's a rarity in the Twin Cities to find three nicely renovated Victorian commercial buildings in a row, as is the case here. The Rochat Block, the prettiest of the trio, was commissioned by a Swiss-born watchmaker named George Rochat. The Louise was built by William G. Robertson as an income property and named after his wife and daughter. The Sauerwein Block, which once had a large Odd Fellows lodge hall on its top floor, was constructed for a saloonkeeper named John Sauerwein. Less ornate than its companions, it was built in the 1890s after the anything-goes Queen Anne style of the previous decade had fallen out of favor.

Irvine Park

The Irvine Park neighborhood, where you'll find some of the oldest houses in St. Paul, is not quite what it seems. Platted in 1849 by John Irvine and Henry Rice, the neighborhood at first glance appears to be a miracle of history—a collection of historic homes within shouting distance of downtown that has somehow remained largely intact for a period of more than 150 years. To be sure, there are houses here that still stand on their original sites, and the little park itself—the only New England–style square in the Twin Cities—is indeed a wonderful survivor from another time.

But the neighborhood as a whole can best be described as a historic reconstruction, initiated in the 1970s by a determined band of residents who worked with the St. Paul Housing and Redevelopment Authority and other agencies to transform what had become a very blighted part of the city. A restoration plan guided the transformation, which occurred under the direction of a design review committee. Although some buildings were razed, many of the most historic homes were restored. Several houses—either from within the neighborhood or from more distant locales—were moved onto vacant lots. The plan also included new infill development designed, with varying degrees of success, to complement the neighborhood's historic character.

Much of the neighborhood was added to the National Register of Historic Places in 1973 and is also a city-designated historic district. Today, Irvine Park is a vibrant community, fiercely defended by its politically astute residents, who take rightful pride in the work that went into preserving it.

Irvine Park

POI D Irvine Park N *L*

Walnut St. and Ryan Ave.

1849 and later / renovated,
William Sanders, 1978

This small square, laid out so that streets radiate from the center of each side, was for its first 20 years or so little more than an unnamed patch of open ground used to graze livestock. The city finally began to develop the park in 1872, the year in which it was named after pioneer John Irvine. A fountain was installed in 1881, but beyond that very little was done to improve the park. By the 1970s, when the neighborhood's renaissance began, the fountain was long gone and the park as a whole was in disrepair. That soon changed, however: in 1978 a new fountain replicating the original was installed in the center of the park, which was also landscaped to more closely resemble its nineteenth-century appearance.

16 Murray-Lanpher House N *L*

35 Irvine Pk.

Edward P. Bassford, 1886

Irvine Park's grand Victorian dame, restored in the 1970s after enduring many years as an asphalt-sided hulk cut up into numerous sleeping rooms. This is probably what most people have in mind when they dream of a Queen Anne house.

17 Wagner-Marty House N *L*

38 Irvine Pk.

ca. 1858

This lot's complex history provides a perfect example of how Irvine Park was re-created. The handsome Greek Revival house you see today was built in the 1850s in what is now suburban Woodbury. It was moved here in the early 1980s after a house transplanted to this site in 1979 (from St. Paul's East Side) burned down. Before all of this happened, there were at least two other houses here, including a spectacular Queen Anne razed in 1968.

18 Elizabeth Robbins House N *L*

40 Irvine Pk.

Mould and McNicol, 1888

A fairly simple Victorian that's hard to assign to one stylistic camp or another.

19 William and Marie Antoinette Spencer House N *L*

47 Irvine Pk.

1860

Greek Revival but with a hint of the lacy Victorian styles to come.

Wright-Prendergast House

20 Wright-Prendergast House N *L*

223 Walnut St.

1851 / 1860 / remodeled, Mark Fitzpatrick, 1907

A fairly simple Greek Revival house that took on far grander aspirations when its second owners, James and Anna Prendergast, hired architect Mark Fitzpatrick to add some neoclassical heft to the main facade. Fitzpatrick obliged with a monumental Ionic portico crowned by an ornate pediment. It's not quite Tara, but it'll do for St. Paul. Descendants of the Prendergasts still live in the house.

21 Henry and Fanny Horn House N L

50 Irvine Pk.

1869 / addition, Augustus Gauger, 1881 / rebuilt, Greg Hotzler, ca. 1980

A house shaped by interventions and accidents. It started out as a small vernacular specimen in 1869. Twelve years later, new owners, Henry and Fanny Horn, hired Augustus Gauger to design a large addition. More changes came in the 1970s when the house was converted into a duplex. After a fire ravaged the older portion of the home in 1980, it was reconstructed yet again. What might happen next is anyone's guess.

22 Eaton-Myler House N L

53 Irvine Pk.

1853

Another very old house, built for a carpenter named Alonzo Eaton and in 1981 moved here from its original site, about six blocks away on Forbes St.

23 John McDonald House N L

56 Irvine Pk.

1873

The front of this Italianate house has so much going on that it looks downright crowded. Now condominiums, the house was moved from Smith Ave. in 1978 and restored. Legend holds that it's the only house in St. Paul history to receive a parking ticket, issued by an eagle-eyed enforcement agent when the structure was left in the street overnight during its move.

24 Dr. Justus Ohage House N L

59 Irvine Pk.

Emil Ulrici, 1889

There's a decidedly German feel to this large Romanesque Revival house, built of cream-colored brick and supposedly designed to resemble the childhood home of Ohage's wife, Augusta, in St. Louis.

Dr. Justus Ohage House

She had little time to enjoy her new home, however, dying at age 34 just weeks after the house was finished. Notable features include a polygonal corner tower worthy of a small church and a porte cochere made of cast iron.

Its owner was more remarkable than the house. After his wife's premature death, Ohage raised their five children, established St. Paul's public health service, equipped the public baths at Harriet Island before donating them to the city, and also found time to perform the first successful gall bladder operation in the United States, in 1886.

25 Humphrey-Willis House N L

240 Ryan Ave.

1851 / addition, 1885

The original portion of this house is a perfectly symmetrical version of a hip-roofed Georgian house, shrunk to cottage size.

26 Charles Symonds House N L

234 Ryan Ave.

1850

This simple box of a house is thought to be the oldest in St. Paul. It was built by Charles Symonds, a Scotsman and former sea captain who'd wandered far from salt water. Originally across the street and just to the east, the house was moved to this location by a new owner in

Charles Symonds House

1913. The front porches were rebuilt in 1975 when the house was converted into a duplex.

27 Panama Flat Condominiums N *L*

Irvine Pk. and Ryan Ave.

Lilyholm Young and Associates, 1980

Though these wood-sheathed condominiums aren't to everyone's taste, they're far more interesting than the brick boxes often built in historic districts today.

Jay and Henry Knox House

28 Jay and Henry Knox House N *L*

26 Irvine Pk.

1860

Built by brothers who were both bankers, this is the only Gothic Revival house in Irvine Park and one of the few left in the Twin Cities. The vertical board-and-batten siding, a hallmark of the style, was discovered beneath a stucco overlay when new owners began restoring the house in the 1970s.

29 Parker-Marshall House N *L*

30 Irvine Pk.

1852

This fine side-hall Greek Revival house, the oldest facing the park, was originally at 35 Irvine Pk. In 1883 it was moved to an adjoining lot and reoriented. It took another short trip in 1976 when it was moved to this site, after

Parker-Marshall House

which the new owners spent six years restoring it. Past residents include William Marshall, governor of Minnesota from 1866 to 1870.

30 Simpson-Wood House N *L*

32 Irvine Pk.

ca. 1853 / addition, ca. 1865

A simple Federal Style house. Like the Jansen house (below), it once stood on Sherman St.; it joined the Irvine Park neighborhood in 1978.

31 Frank Jansen House N *L*

310 Ryan Ave.

1908

Frank Jansen built this house as an investment. Originally on Sherman St., it was moved here in 1980.

32 Rogers-Johnson House N *L*

306 South Exchange St.

Augustus Gauger, 1881

Another stylistic combo, built by a man named William Dice Rogers, who years earlier had gained considerable notoriety in St. Paul when he paid a visit to his neighbor's wife while somehow neglecting to wear pants. Rogers's apparel problems apparently continued: his second wife divorced him on grounds of infidelity.

Near West Side

33 Wiesinger House N L

304 South Exchange St.

ca. 1880

An impressive brick French Second Empire house that once stood on this lot was torn down after a fire in 1978. This house was moved here four years later from its original site at 411 Selby Ave. It is now three condominiums.

34 Stilwell-Hankey House N L

310 Sherman St.

1853 / additions, ca. 1905, 1915

A simple wooden box with several additions. It was converted to offices in the 1980s.

35 Otto and Marie Dreher House N L

300 South Exchange St.

1881

A transitional design, hovering between the Italianate of the 1870s and the Eastlake of the early 1880s. Otto Dreher was a German immigrant who belonged to no fewer than six singing societies and had quite a funeral procession when he died in 1889. The house, originally on Ramsey St., was moved here in 1982.

36 Second Frank Jansen House N L

278–80 Sherman St.

1911

Only in St. Paul would you find a house that carries an address on a nonexistent street. When it was built by the busy Frank Jansen, the house—notable for its two-story front porch—was indeed on Sherman. However, portions of the street were vacated in the 1970s. Despite this irksome fact, the house retained its address.

LOST 2 *When the famed First Minnesota Regiment returned from the Civil War, its members were feted at a meeting hall known as the* **Athenaeum** *that once occupied this site. The Athenaeum burned down in 1886.*

37 Knox-Austin-Rogers House N L

284 South Exchange St.

James Knox Taylor and Matthew Craig, 1885

A restored Queen Anne house designed by architect James Knox Taylor, who would soon become Cass Gilbert's first partner. Horace Austin, Minnesota's governor from 1870 to 1874, lived here for a time.

38 Forepaugh's Restaurant (Joseph Forepaugh House) N L

276 South Exchange St.

1870 / enlarged, Abraham M. Radcliffe, ca. 1880 / renovated, 1976

One of Irvine Park's best-known attractions, this house-turned-restaurant was built by dry-goods dealer Joseph Forepaugh, who made enough money supplying troops during the Civil War to

Forepaugh's Restaurant

retire at the unripe age of 34. The house's next owner, Gen. John Hammond, was more directly involved in the war, serving as Gen. William Sherman's chief of staff. Parts of the mansion, including the front half of the mansard roof and the porte cochere, are modern reconstructions.

Alexander Ramsey House

39 Alexander Ramsey House ! N L

265 South Exchange St.

Monroe Sheire, 1872

This hefty stone house is the finest surviving example in the Twin Cities of the French Second Empire style. Although not as large as the fabulous St. Paul mansions of the 1880s and later, the house conveys a sense of rugged grandeur that remains impressive to this day.

Alexander Ramsey was Minnesota's first territorial governor and second state governor. His first house, built in 1850 on the same site, was far more modest. In 1857 he and his wife, Anna, moved it across Walnut St. with the intention of building a much larger new home here. But it wasn't until 1868—by which time Ramsey was a member of the U.S. Senate—that he and Anna were finally able to start work on their "mansion house," as they called it. Construction took four years, and when the house was finally finished in late 1872, the Ramseys were so pleased that they threw a party for the 25 or so laborers who had worked on the project, even providing ten gallons of beer to keep things lively.

Built of blocks of local limestone, the house offers a catalog of French Second Empire features, including a mansard roof, paired eaves brackets, window hoods (a holdover from the closely related Italianate style), and a large front porch with delicate columns and fretwork. The architect, Monroe Sheire, was one of St. Paul's early master builders; he designed a number of mansions (now mostly gone) for the city's elite.

Ramsey's descendants lived in the house until the 1960s, making few changes. In 1964 the mansion and its original furnishings were willed to the Minnesota Historical Society, which restored it inside and out and opened it as a house museum. The house's large grounds have also remained intact, although the carriage house is a modern reconstruction of the original.

40 John and Elizabeth Matheis House N L

307 Walnut St.

ca. 1853 / enlarged, Augustus Knight, 1874

Now condominiums, this large house started out as a much smaller Greek Revival home. It was enlarged in the 1870s and given an Italianate look. The tower is a modern reconstruction.

41 McCloud-Edgerton House N L

311 Walnut St.

ca. 1867

An unusual one-story house with Greek Revival and Italianate features. Built as a duplex, it was until 1916 located at 240 West Seventh St.

42 Panama Flats Row House (Stoddart Block) N L

226–34 South Exchange St.

George and Frank Orff, 1886

Originally known as the Stoddart Block, this Queen Anne–style row house was renamed Panama Flats in 1907 by owners who were apparently enthralled by the Panama Canal, then under construction. The building was rehabilitated into condominiums in 1979.

Near West Side

Armstrong-Quinlan House

43 Armstrong-Quinlan House N *L*

225 Eagle Pkwy.

Edward P. Bassford, 1886 / renovated, 2006

A 10,000-square-foot double house, originally located at 233–35 West Fifth St. in downtown St. Paul. It was built as a rental property by John M. Armstrong, whose brother was Minnesota's first territorial treasurer. Architect Edward P. Bassford gave it the full Victo-

rian treatment, layering the front facade with arches, pediments, turrets, finials, and a dizzying variety of other decorative flourishes.

Converted into the Quinlan Nursing Home in 1940, the house eventually became downtown's last Victorian-era dwelling, standing in lonely splendor in a sea of parking lots. In 1988 the State of Minnesota purchased the house for possible use as an arts high school. That idea never materialized, however, and the house stood vacant for 13 years while a blizzard of studies, plans, reports, and proposals piled up around it. In 2001 the house was moved at a cost of $2 million to its current site, where the Historic Irvine Park Association and the West Seventh/Fort Road Federation turned it into upscale condominiums. Whether the expenditure of so much public money to provide housing for a few wealthy people makes sense is a question worth considering.

The Upper Landing (Upper Levee)

Located near the foot of Chestnut Street beneath Irvine Park, these river flats once harbored a steamboat landing. Because of the annual threat of flooding, the area wasn't considered desirable for housing, but that didn't stop an Italian immigrant community from thriving here for many years. Today, a fancy new apartment and condominium development occupies most of the site.

POI E Chicago, Milwaukee, St. Paul and Pacific Railroad (Milwaukee Road) "Short Line"

Along Mississippi River cliffs west of Chestnut St.

1879 and later

The rail line that climbs the cliffs here is probably the steepest in the Twin Cities, rising 230 feet in its first five miles. The project, which required construction of massive stone walls, was one of the great engineering feats of nineteenth-century St. Paul. The Milwaukee Road built this "short line" between St. Paul and Minneapolis to shave a few miles from the standard intercity route through Trout Brook valley east of Lowertown. The tracks are

now used by the Canadian Pacific Railroad.

44 St. Paul Municipal Grain Terminal (Equity Cooperative) Head House and Sack House (City House) N

266 Old Shepard Rd.

George M. Shepard, John W. Kelsey, and Walter F. Schulz (engineers), 1931 / renovated, 2009

These two buildings—a tall concrete grain elevator and an adjoining sack house—are all that remain of the old St. Paul Municipal Grain Terminal. The terminal, designed to transfer grain from railroad cars to barges, originally connected to a flour mill and a large elevator complex built by the farmer-owned Equity

Little Italy, 1908

Cooperative Exchange. The idea was to provide a means of shipping grain other than through Minneapolis, where such giant firms as Cargill controlled the trade.

Shipment by river became feasible in the 1930s when the U.S. Army Corps of Engineers built a system of locks and dams to provide a nine-foot-deep navigation channel on the Mississippi. The terminal complex, which handled 17 million bushels of grain a year by the late 1930s, gradually grew obsolete, and most of the structures were demolished in 1989. The head house and sack house were added to the National Register of Historic Places in 2004. The buildings, renovated in 2009 at a cost of $2 million, now serve as a park pavilion and gathering place along the regional trail here.

LOST 3 *Much lore surrounds the immigrant community known as* **"Little Italy"** *that once flourished on the Upper Levee Flats along the Mississippi River west of Chestnut St. The flood-prone flats were first settled in the nineteenth century by a mixed lot of squatters, mainly poor immigrants. Displaying the usual sensitivity of the era, a newspaper reporter in 1886 described these newcomers as suffering from "stinted intellects, depraved habits, and a lawless disposition," among other alleged deficiencies.*

By 1900, immigrants from two small towns in southern Italy established themselves on the flats and gradually constructed a community of tidy owner-built homes that survived for 60 years despite numerous inundations. A particularly bad flood in 1952 finally convinced the city to clear the flats. The last of the old houses was demolished in 1960, after which the city—in a move that cannot be described as visionary—turned over the site to a large scrap yard. By 1990, however, St. Paul was no longer enamored of junk on the riverfront, and the flats were once again cleared, paving the way for development of new housing and parks.

45 Upper Landing Development

Shepard Rd. west of Chestnut St.

KKE Architects and ESG Architects, 2003 and later

Upper Landing Development

Here on the old flood-washed flats of the former Little Italy is one of the largest housing developments in St. Paul's history, carefully protected from any threat of architectural excellence by the city's design guidelines. The project consists of seven large housing blocks that contain more than 600 townhomes, condominiums, and rental apartments. Arranged with all the charm of military barracks, the brick-, stucco-, and metal-clad buildings could have gone anywhere, and you have to wonder after looking at this development whether the city should seriously consider ditching its "new urbanist" guidelines in favor of a design process open to a broader range of possibilities. Although the architecture here leaves much to be desired, the city did its usual first-class job of laying out new parks, trails, and other public amenities as part of the development.

Annotated Bibliography

Adams, John S., and Barbara J. VanDrasek. *Minneapolis–St. Paul: People, Place and Public Life*. Minneapolis: University of Minnesota Press, 1993. Written by two geographers, this book provides a useful overview of the growth and development of the Twin Cities.

Anderes, Fred, and Ann Agranoff. *Ice Palaces*. New York: Abbeyville Press, 1983. Includes two chapters on St. Paul's many ice palaces.

Anderson, David, ed. *Downtown: A History of Downtown Minneapolis and Downtown St. Paul in the Words of the People Who Lived It*. Minneapolis: Nodin Press, 2000. Good stories about the days when the two downtowns were truly at the center of life in the Twin Cities.

Bennett, Edward H., William E. Parson, and George Herrold. *Plan of St. Paul: The Capital City of Minnesota*. [St. Paul]: Commissioner of Public Works, 1922. Not nearly as grand as its Minneapolis counterpart, but it does offer some intriguing insights into how planners of the era hoped to change St. Paul for the better (mostly, they failed).

Besse, Kirk. *Show Houses, Twin Cities Style*. Minneapolis: Victoria Publications, 1997. A history of St. Paul and Minneapolis movie theaters.

Blodgett, Geoffrey. *Cass Gilbert: The Early Years*. St. Paul: Minnesota Historical Society Press, 2001. Much information about the early St. Paul career of the man who designed the Minnesota State Capitol and many other monuments.

A Brief History of the Irvine Park District: The People and Architecture of an Extraordinary Neighborhood. St. Paul: Historic Irvine Park Association, 1986. A nicely illustrated pamphlet that covers all of the historic structures in one of St. Paul's oldest neighborhoods.

Castle, Henry A. *History of St. Paul and Vicinity: A Chronicle of Progress*. 3 vols. Chicago and New York: Lewis Publishing Co., 1912. An encyclopedic work that amply displays the biases of its era. But it's an enjoyable read (in spots) and offers much information not readily available elsewhere.

Christen, Barbara S., and Steven Flanders. *Cass Gilbert, Life and Work: Architect of the Public Domain*. New York: Norton, 2001. Includes a chapter on Gilbert's career in St. Paul.

Conforti, Michael, ed. *Art and Life on the Upper Mississippi, 1890–1915: Minnesota 1900*. Newark: University of Delaware Press, 1994. Includes chapters on turn-of-the-century Minnesota architecture and a long essay on the work of Purcell and Elmslie.

Diers, John W., and Aaron Isaacs. *Twin Cities by Trolley: The Streetcar Era in Minneapolis and St. Paul*. Minneapolis: University of Minnesota Press, 2007. The fullest account available of the streetcar system that did much to shape downtown St. Paul and the rest of the Twin Cities.

Discover St. Paul: A Short History of Seven St. Paul Neighborhoods. St. Paul: Ramsey County Historical Society, 1979. Historical sketches illustrated with maps and photographs.

Earhart, Andrew G. *The Buildings of Saint Paul: The Mears Park Area*. St. Paul: The Author, 1992. Information on every building that faces the historic Lowertown park.

Eaton, Leonard K. *Gateway Cities and Other Essays*. Ames: Iowa State University Press, 1989. Includes a chapter on warehouses in St. Paul.

Empson, Donald L. *The Street Where You Live: A Guide to the Place Names of St. Paul*. 1975. Minneapolis: University of Minnesota Press, 2006. If you've ever wondered how St. Paul acquired so many unusual street names, you'll find the answers here.

Frame, Robert M. III. *James J. Hill's St. Paul: A Guide.* St. Paul: James J. Hill Reference Library, 1988. Identifies various St. Paul buildings associated with the fabled Empire Builder.

Gebhard, David, and Tom Martinson. *A Guide to the Architecture of Minnesota.* Minneapolis: University of Minnesota Press, 1977. Now badly dated, this remains the only comprehensive guide of its kind. The chapters on the Twin Cities omit many significant buildings in St. Paul.

Hampl, Patricia, and Dave Page, eds. *The St. Paul Stories of F. Scott Fitzgerald.* St. Paul: Borealis Books, 2004. Some of Fitzgerald's most famous stories focused on his early years in St. Paul, and they're all here, collected for the first time in one volume. Hampl's introduction is superb.

Harris, Moira. *Fire & Ice: The History of the St. Paul Winter Carnival.* St. Paul: Pogo Press, 2003. Much information on early ice palaces and other carnival structures.

Hennessy, William B. *Past and Present of St. Paul, Minnesota.* Chicago: S. J. Clarke Publishing Co., 1906. A big subscription book offering lots of secondhand information with a few good photographs.

Hess, Jeffrey A., and Paul Clifford Larson. *St. Paul Architecture: A History.* Minneapolis: University of Minnesota Press, 2006. The most thorough account of St. Paul's architectural history available. The chapter on Period Revival architecture is especially good.

Irish, Sharon. *Cass Gilbert, Architect: Modern Traditionalist.* New York: Monacelli Press, 1999. A biography of Minnesota's most famous architect.

Johnson, Frederick L., and David Thofern. *The Skyway Tour of Saint Paul History.* St. Paul: St. Paul Foundation and Minnesota Historical Society, 1991. A pamphlet describing historic sites and buildings that can be seen from the skyways.

Kane, Sister Joan, and Paul D. Nelson. *Rocky Roots: Geology and Stone Construction in Downtown St. Paul.* 2nd ed. St. Paul: Ramsey County Historical Society, 2008. A handy, well-written guide to the many types of stone used for downtown St. Paul buildings.

Kenney, Dave. *Twin Cities Album: A Visual History.* St. Paul: Minnesota Historical Society Press, 2005. A nice array of photographs and other images that provide an overview of the history of Minneapolis and St. Paul. There's also an informative text.

Koeper, H. F. *Historic St. Paul Buildings.* St. Paul: City Planning Board, 1964. This booklet, published as the preservation movement was just getting under way, identified nearly 100 St. Paul buildings thought to be historically and architecturally significant. Alas, not all of them survived the 1960s.

Kudalis, Eric, ed. *100 Places Plus 1: An Unofficial Architectural Survey of Favorite Minnesota Sites.* Minneapolis: AIA Minnesota, 1996. Various essayists describe their favorite buildings and places in Minnesota.

Kunz, Virginia. *The Mississippi and St. Paul: A Short History of the City's 150-Year Love Affair with Its River.* St. Paul: Ramsey County Historical Society, 1987. A brief but informative look at how the Mississippi River shaped St. Paul's development and vice versa.

———. *St. Paul: Saga of an American City.* Woodland Hills, CA: Windsor Publications, 1977. A glossy "corporate history" that tends to plow familiar ground.

Larson, Paul Clifford. *Minnesota Architect: The Life and Work of Clarence H. Johnston*. Afton, MN: Afton Historical Society Press, 1996. A detailed study of Johnston, who designed numerous important buildings in St. Paul. Includes a complete catalog of his work.

Larson, Paul Clifford, with Susan Brown, eds. *The Spirit of H. H. Richardson on the Midland Prairies: Regional Transformations of an Architectural Style*. Minneapolis and Ames: University of Minnesota Art Museum and Iowa State University Press, 1988. A series of essays examining the influence, in the Twin Cities and elsewhere, of the great Boston architect Henry Hobson Richardson.

Lathrop, Alan. *Churches of Minnesota: An Illustrated Guide*. Minneapolis: University of Minnesota Press, 2003. Includes information about a number of significant churches in St. Paul.

Lindley, John M. *Celebrate St. Paul: 150 Years of History*. Encino, CA: Cherbo Publishing Group, 2003. The latest history of St. Paul, profusely illustrated.

Maccabee, Paul. *John Dillinger Slept Here: A Crooks' Tour of Crime and Corruption in St. Paul, 1920–1936*. St. Paul: Minnesota Historical Society Press, 1995. Everything you ever wanted to know about St. Paul's gangster era in the 1920s and 1930s. Includes excellent maps.

Martin, Judith, and Antony Goddard. *Past Choices/Present Landscapes: The Impact of Urban Renewal on the Twin Cities*. Minneapolis: Center for Urban and Regional Affairs, 1989. A straightforward account of how urban renewal dramatically altered St. Paul and Minneapolis.

Martin, Judith, and David Lanegran. *Where We Live: The Residential Districts of Minneapolis and Saint Paul*. Minneapolis: University of Minnesota Press, 1983. Lots of good information about a wide variety of neighborhoods.

McAlester, Virginia, and Lee McAlester. *A Field Guide to American Houses*. New York: Alfred A. Knopf, 1984. Obviously this isn't a work about the Twin Cities, but it is a superb guidebook, with excellent drawings and photographs to help you identify the style of almost any kind of house.

McClure, Harlan E. *A Guide to the Architecture of the Twin Cities: Minneapolis and St. Paul, 1820–1955*. New York: Reinhold Publishing Co., 1955. Outdated, but interesting for its take on the first generation of "modern" architecture here.

Millett, Larry. *AIA Guide to the Twin Cities: The Essential Source on the Architecture of Minneapolis and St. Paul*. St. Paul: Minnesota Historical Society Press, 2007. Includes a chapter on downtown St. Paul.

———. *Lost Twin Cities*. St. Paul: Minnesota Historical Society Press, 1992. A look at the Twin Cities' many vanished buildings.

———. *Strange Days, Dangerous Nights: Photos from the Speed Graphic Era*. St. Paul: Borealis Books, 2004. Newspaper photographs from St. Paul in the 1940s and 1950s that contain much lurid gore but also show what the city looked like before the age of urban renewal.

Millett, Larry (with photographs by Jerry Mathiason). *Twin Cities Then and Now*. St. Paul: Minnesota Historical Society Press, 1996. Historic photographs of more than 70 street scenes paired with new pictures taken from the same locations.

Murphy, Patricia, and Susan Granger. *Historic Sites Survey of Saint Paul and Ramsey County, 1980–1983: Final Report*. St. Paul: St. Paul Heritage Preservation Commission and Ramsey County Historical Society, 1983. A survey of significant architecture in St. Paul and Ramsey County. The report contains errors and omissions, but it's an invaluable reference document.

Newson, Thomas N. *Pen Sketches of St. Paul, Minnesota, and Biographical Sketches of Old Settlers, from the Earliest Settlement of the City, up to and including the Year 1857.* St. Paul: The Author, 1886. The title says it all. A big, quirky book that is usually interesting and in places downright amusing.

Nord, Mary Ann, comp. *The National Register of Historic Places in Minnesota.* St. Paul: Minnesota Historical Society Press, 2003. Lists every Minnesota building on the register.

Olson, Russell L. *The Electric Railways of Minnesota.* Hopkins: Minnesota Transportation Museum, 1977. Written by a trolley buff, this study describes in sometimes numbing detail the Twin Cities' late, great streetcar system.

Peterson, Richard, and Paul Clifford Larson. *Terra Cotta in the Twin Cities.* St. Paul: Northern Clay Center, 1993. A guide to buildings adorned with terra-cotta, which was widely used as an architectural material between 1880 and 1930.

Poppeliers, John C., S. Allen Chambers, Jr., and Nancy B. Schwartz. *What Style Is It? A Guide to American Architecture.* 1983. Rev. ed., Washington, DC: Preservation Press, ca. 2002. A useful guidebook that includes photographs, drawings, a glossary of terms, and a good bibliography.

Pyle, J. G., ed. *Picturesque St. Paul.* St. Paul: Northwestern Photo Co., 1888. Great photographs of old-time St. Paul, assembled by the man who wrote the first biography of James J. Hill.

Richards, Hanje. *Minneapolis–St. Paul Then and Now.* San Diego, CA: Thunder Bay Press, 2001. Lots of photographs, but the text isn't especially good.

Richter, Bonnie, ed. *Saint Paul Omnibus: Images of the Changing City.* St. Paul: Old Town Restorations, Inc., 1979. A nice booklet that explores the city's architectural history.

Sandeen, Ernest. *St. Paul's Historic Summit Avenue.* 1978. Minneapolis: University of Minnesota Press, 2004. Although Sandeen's architectural judgments are a bit eccentric, this book is a delight to read and remains the best guide to St. Paul's most famous thoroughfare, which once extended well into downtown.

Schmid, Calvin F. *Social Saga of Two Cities: An Ecological and Statistical Study of Social Trends in Minneapolis and St. Paul.* Minneapolis: Council of Social Agencies, Bureau of Social Research, 1937. Conceived as a Depression-era project, this is one of the most informative books ever written about the Twin Cities. Especially valuable are the superb maps and charts.

Schulyer, Montgomery. *American Architecture and Other Writings.* William H. Jordy and Ralph Coe, eds. Cambridge, MA: Harvard University Press, Belknap Press, 1961. Schuyler was an outstanding turn-of-the-century architecture critic. Includes a fascinating 1891 essay on buildings in St. Paul and Minneapolis.

Slade, George Richard. *Banking in the Great Northern Territory: An Illustrated History.* Afton, MN: Afton Historical Society Press, 2005. A regional history that includes photographs and descriptions of several old downtown bank buildings.

Taylor, David Vassar, and Paul Clifford Larson. *Cap Wigington: An Architectural Legacy in Ice and Stone.* St. Paul: Minnesota Historical Society Press, 2001. A good account of the life and work of St. Paul's first black architect.

Trent, Vera. *Tracing the Steps of Historic St. Paul.* St. Paul: St. Paul Foundation, 1991. A downtown walking tour with emphasis on the city's early history.

Trimble, Steve. *Historic Photos of St. Paul.* Nashville, TN: Turner Publishing Co., 2008. A good selection of photographs, including many taken in downtown St. Paul.

Vincent, Jeanne Anne. "St. Paul Architecture, 1848–1906." Master's thesis, University of Minnesota, 1944. An early study of St. Paul's historic architecture. Includes many photographs.

Warner, George E., and Charles M. Foote, comps. *History of Ramsey County and the City of St. Paul, including the Explorers and Pioneers of Minnesota, by Edward D. Neill, and Outlines of the History of Minnesota, by J. Fletcher Williams.* Minneapolis: North Star Publishing Co., 1881. A useful compendium, even if the title seems nearly as long as the book.

Westbrook, Nicolas, ed. *A Guide to the Industrial Archaeology of the Twin Cities.* St. Paul and Minneapolis: Society for Industrial Archaeology, 1983. Fascinated by bridges, dams, factories, railroad yards, and the like? If so, you'll enjoy this guide.

Westbrook, Virginia. *Historic Lowertown: A Walking Tour.* St. Paul: St. Paul Heritage Preservation Commission, 1988. If you're interested in taking a stroll around the historic Lowertown warehouse district, this pamphlet will come in handy.

Williams, J. Fletcher. *A History of the City of Saint Paul to 1875.* 1887. St. Paul: Minnesota Historical Society, 1983. A good "snack" book, filled with colorful stories of early St. Paul.

Wingerd, Mary Lethert. *Claiming the City: Politics, Faith, and the Power of Place in St. Paul.* Ithaca, NY: Cornell University Press, 2001. One of the best books ever written about St. Paul. It offers a convincing explanation for why St. Paul is in many ways so different from Minneapolis.

Index

Every building and site described in the Guide is listed as a primary entry in the index, both by previous and current names. Some street names beginning with "North," "South," "East," or "West" are inverted and alphabetized under the keyword part of the street name (e.g., "East Fifth Street" is alphabetized as "Fifth St. East"). Building and street names beginning with numbers are alphabetized as if spelled out. The names of people, firms, organizations, and government offices involved in creating the works listed in the Guide appear in Upper and Lower Case Small Caps. Unless otherwise indicated, they are architects, associated artists, or builders. Names of geographic areas or communities within the greater Twin Cities appear in **boldface italic**. A page reference in **boldface** indicates a photograph of the building, area, or other work.

The following abbreviations appear in the index:

Admin.	Administration	Co.	Company	Ins.	Insurance
Amer.	American	Condos.	Condominiums	MN	Minnesota
Apts.	Apartments	Corp.	Corporation	Mpls.	Minneapolis
Assn.	Association	Ct.	Court	Natl.	National
Assocs.	Associates	Dept.	Department	RR	Railroad/Railway
Bldg.	Building	H.S.	High School	St.	Street
Bros.	Brothers	Hosp.	Hospital	Univ.	University

Picture Credits